PENGUIN VEER
UNDAUNTED

Bhaavna Arora is the bestselling author of four books, a teacher, an educationist and a corporate trainer. Bhaavna dons many hats, but at the core of it, she is deeply devoted to the Indian Armed Forces, and equally passionate about penning down their true stories and life experiences. She is an Indian who is in awe of the bravery and courage shown by the Indian Army in dire times.

Writing is akin to breathing for her, and she embraces life afresh with every story. Her works reflect the intensity, depth of research and involvement she pours into every word.

In writing this book, Bhaavna has travelled back in time with those close to Lt Ummer Fayaz, feeling their pain and loss. This book is an honest attempt to glorify and celebrate the life of this brave heart.

PRAISE FOR THE BOOK

'Through her story, Bhaavna has made Lt Ummer Fayaz come alive. And in this revelation we see not only more of the man, but also the environment in which he lived and how this shaped his life and ultimately his death. Bhaavna has truthfully conveyed all she witnessed, and in this lies the real value of the book'—**Lieutenant General Deependra Singh Hooda, PVSM, UYSM, AVSM, VSM and Bar, ADC (retd), former general officer commanding-in-chief, Northern Command, Indian Army**

'It is a matter of pride that Bhaavna Arora has chosen to relate the story of Lt Ummer Fayaz, a young Kashmiri who chose to join the Indian Army despite the challenges it posed to him and his family. This inspired several fellow Kashmiris trapped in the vicious cycle of violence to seek a new path. His gruesome death, while he was on holiday to attend a wedding in the family, was a veritable tragedy, something that must make all Indians hang their heads in shame. That a young boy, with stars in his eyes and enthusiasm in every act, was struck down in the prime of his life is a reminder that the problem of Kashmir concerns all of us and to solve it is our collective responsibility. *Undaunted* is an attempt to portray the reality of Kashmir as also its human side. I would recommend all those who are interested in the idea of a strong, powerful and just India to read the book'—**Lt Gen. Satish Dua, PVSM, UYSM, SM, VSM (retd), GOC 15 Corps during the surgical strikes**

'This book is a befitting tribute to the memory of a national martyr who dared to don the army uniform conscious of the dangers involved. It is written with a rare sensitivity that would inspire many Kashmiris to serve their country in the face of all odds. I particularly liked the manner in which the author has narrated Ummer Fayaz's story, interspersed with her personal experiences of Kashmir as she went about researching her book. It's a must-read for all who care about Kashmir and its future, and for those Kashmiris who refuse to be cowed down by terror threats when it comes to serving their country'—**Neeraj Kumar, former commissioner of police, Delhi; former DGP, Goa; former DGP (Prisons), Delhi; former head, Anti-Corruption and Security Unit, Board of Control for Cricket in India; and former joint director, CBI**

'What can you say about a twenty-three-year-old boy who died? That he was brave and patriotic, that he had the courage to swim against the tide, that he could display love as only soldiers can and could understand in his young mind the contradictions of the situation any local-sponsored conflict throws up'—**Lt Gen. S.A. Hasnain, PVSM, UYSM, AVSM, SM, VSM and Bar (retd), former GOC 15 Corps and former military secretary of the Indian Army**

'This is not just a book about Lt Ummer Fayaz. It is a book about the Indian Army. It is a book about the people of Kashmir. It is a book about the love and heartbreak of a family. And it is a book about heroes'—**Maj. Gaurav Arya (retd), editor-in-chief, Chanakya Forum**

'Writing the story of a martyr cannot be easy. More so, if the martyr is someone like Lt Ummer Fayaz, a man who sought to live not only for himself and his family, but also for his community, region and motherland.

Lt Ummer was a man of aspiration and noble intent. He was also a man unafraid of taking risks. Going against the dominant view of his region, he joined the army. There, he strove to reach the heights of excellence. After being commissioned as an officer, a life of achievement and recognition lay before him. It was cut brutally short through a senseless act of violence, which sadly, the nation has come to associate with the Kashmir Valley. Still, Lt Ummer's short life holds our attention for the hope that it embodied and the promise it held'—**Maj. Dr Surendra Poonia, VSM (retd), Limca Book of Records record holder; physician and former Special Forces officer, Indian Army; and founder, Soldierathon marathon and Fit Bharat**

'This book takes you through not just the life of Lt Ummer but it builds around you the facts about Kashmir, its existing state, the psychology of kids, families, soldiers and their perspective towards militancy and militants'—**Maj. D.P. Singh (retd), India's first blade runner and Kargil War hero**

UNDAUNTED
LT UMMER FAYAZ OF KASHMIR

bhaavna arora

PENGUIN
VEER
An imprint of Penguin Random House

PENGUIN VEER

Penguin Veer is an imprint of the Penguin Random House group of companies whose addresses can be found at global.penguinrandomhouse.com

Published by Penguin Random House India Pvt. Ltd
4th Floor, Capital Tower 1, MG Road,
Gurugram 122 002, Haryana, India

Penguin
Random House
India

First published by Westland Publications Pvt. Ltd in 2019
Published in Penguin Veer by Penguin Random House India 2024

ISBN 9780143470892

Typeset in Adobe Caslon Pro by MAP Systems, Bengaluru, India
Printed at Replika Press Pvt. Ltd, India

www.penguin.co.in

MIX
Paper | Supporting
responsible forestry
FSC™ C016779

Contents

Foreword   ix
A Note to My Readers   xi
Prologue   xiii

Chapter 1   1
Chapter 2   10
Chapter 3   31
Chapter 4   48
Chapter 5   53
Chapter 6   66
Chapter 7   81
Chapter 8   102
Chapter 9   122
Chapter 10   136
Chapter 11   144
Chapter 12   165
Chapter 13   174
Chapter 14   191
Chapter 15   196
Chapter 16   219

Epilogue   241

सेनाध्यक्ष

CHIEF OF THE ARMY STAFF

Foreword

Undaunted: Lt Ummer Fayaz of Kashmir is not only the story of a valiant Kashmiri lad but also a reflection of an indomitable and time-tested institution, the Indian Army.

Ummer Fayaz was the young man from Kashmir who chose to remain loyal to his duty even at the peril of his life. He stood against the extremists as he would stand against the enemy, for the future of his country. While Kashmir oscillates between mundane normalcy and methodical chaos, between dreams and despair, there will always be brave hearts like Ummer Fayaz, who exemplify bravery and devotion to the Nation.

Ummer epitomizes 'Kashmiriyat' in its truest sense and will go down in history as a hero who chose to serve the Nation, against all odds. He became the brave flag-bearer of hope and aspirations of today's Kashmiri youth who dream of a life beyond militancy. The patriotism displayed by Lt Ummer Fayaz will never die and more youth will be motivated by his undaunted spirit and desire to serve the Nation. Ummer Fayaz has not died but has faded away beyond the horizon.

At the heart of the story is also the Indian Army. This book will give you an authentic and detailed account of some of the codes and customs of the Indian Army, an edifice of pluralistic traditions, and how it continues to make efforts to bring about a positive change in Kashmir.

I congratulate the author for having the courage to go into the field and interview the martyrs' families, battle-hardened officers and ordinary people alike. The book not only highlights precious snippets of Lt Ummer's life but also gives a sneak peek into the minds and hearts of a few Kashmiris as also the everyday struggles and joys of army officials in the area. This book is a compelling and deep-felt account, which is sure to immortalize the memory of a remarkable officer in the public conscience.

I wish the author the very best for her future endeavours.

Jai Hind,

Late General Bipin Rawat,
PVSM, UYSM, AVSM, YSM, SM, VSM, ADC,
India's first chief of defence staff,
Indian Army

A Note to My Readers

As a true patriot, I have no business to discriminate one soldier killed in action from the other. And if I could, I would write a story on each one of them. Whether a soldier dies in a terrorist encounter in the Valley, or gets buried in snow at the Siachen glacier, or is shot down by enemy bullets or blown apart by land mines at the border—they all have one thing in common, and that is an unparalleled love for their country. And each of their stories deserves to be told.

The soldiers who died avenging Ummer's killing died no less a valiant death.

This book is dedicated to them and all those who have sacrificed their lives in the line of duty.

Ummer was greatly inspired by Lt Gen. Syed Ata Hasnain because he witnessed his work. If that work deserves appreciation, so does the work of the soldiers who flawlessly executed the surgical strike or conducted successful operations for the elimination of terrorists. It only shows the mettle of the men who have served and continue to serve in these turbulent areas. Col Manu, Col CP, Col Rohit and DSP Ashiq were the few I had the good fortune of meeting.

This book is dedicated to all our brave men in uniform, who serve in the most hostile conditions, while going without meeting their families for months on end.

If only every child were inspired the way Ummer was, no guns would be needed to meet the expectations of Kashmiris. They would then be quite proficient in meeting their own expectations.

This book is also dedicated to every Kashmiri who chooses the high road and sources their inspiration from true patriots.

Last but not least, this book is dedicated to my late grandfather, who served in the Indian Army during the 1962, 1965 and 1971 wars, and my grandmother, who stood beside him like a rock.

Maj. Kamlesh Pandey and Sep. Tenzin Chultim of 62 RR and Gunner Nealesh Singh of 34 RR deserve a special mention in this book, as they sacrificed their lives in avenging Lt Ummer's death.

Prologue

10 May 2017 dawned a regular day for many, barring a few. Shabeer*, hearing a pack of street dogs howl away in the early hours of the morning, was quick to sense that something was amiss. As a cab driver, he liked to make an early start and was usually the first to stand in queue for a token at the taxi stand in Herman Chowk, one of the principal points on the single route connecting Shopian to Kulgam and Anantnag. In a first-come-first-served business, Shabeer knew this would ensure he bagged the first passengers of the day. At 5 a.m. that day, as he approached the stand, Shabeer noticed that the howling dogs were guarding something at the chowk.

As he moved closer, the dogs snarled and barked at him menacingly. There, lying in a pool of blood, was a man. Fear and indecision gripped his heart as he realized he had no idea what to do. Death was hardly unknown to the people of the Kashmir Valley, but Shabeer himself had only seen white-shrouded corpses at funerals till now. That was horrific enough; this was beyond the resources of his imagination.

---

* The names of some persons and places have been changed for security reasons.

His first instinct was to report it, but then, who would invite trouble with the police? He barely eked out a modest living and the last thing he wanted was to be dragged into some controversial investigation. He found himself walking away from the scene as fast as he could. Several other cab drivers who had by now arrived at the taxi stand wondered why he was walking so fast, and that too away from the chowk. Someone called out to him, and Shabeer yelled back, 'There is a dead body at the chowk. Turn around, or the police will question us for hours.' The others too fled immediately.

The next witness was a bread-maker. From a small wheel cart, he made a living by serving early breakfast to cab drivers and a handful of other customers. The sky was just beginning to lighten as he lit his clay oven to make some chai and bread, the only items on his menu in the mornings. That was when he noticed the dogs in the distance. He was amazed that they hadn't come running to him yet, for he would often feed them scraps from his cart. As there were no taxi drivers in sight, he approached the dogs—unafraid, as they knew him well. Then he saw the man lying on the street, his face caked with blood, jaw and mouth disfigured, and a pool of thick, dark blood under him.

Judging by how immobile the body seemed, the bread-maker guessed that the man was dead. He uttered the words, *'Inna lillahi wa inna ilayhi raji'un'* (We belong to Allah and must return to Allah), and turned around to walk to the other end of the chowk, where he knew there'd be more people.

On spotting a few, he said in a shaky voice, 'There's a dead man lying by the chowk. Can you come and see if you recognize him?'

A dozen people accompanied him to the spot, but their first glimpse of the body robbed them of speech for a few moments. After about a minute's silence, they discussed the corpse and remarked on how very young the man seemed. There was a gaping wound in his abdomen as well as injuries to the mouth and jaw, the nature of which they couldn't quite tell because the face was swollen and caked with blood that had dried to a deep crimson. The bread-maker said, 'Should I call the police? I'm an old man, a familiar face in this area; they've known me a long time. They will trust me.'

The others, however, didn't seem too eager to involve the police right away. Someone suggested, 'Chacha, we should call the sarpanch. He is the head of our village and will know what to do.'

The sarpanch, Mushtaq, was accustomed to locals knocking on his door at all hours of the day and night, with tidings of some gruesome atrocity or the other. In the last few years, the news that followed the knocks had rarely been good. And yet, he had never quite got used to it. This time, however, he was in for the shock of his life. Accompanying the others to the chowk, it took him only a moment to recognize whose body it was. 'Ya Allah, this is Ummer! Our Ummer!'

He asked the men to fetch his wife Shakeela, cautioning them not to break the news suddenly to her or reveal any details of what had happened. No doubt she would be devastated by the mere thought, leave aside the sight, of their beloved nephew—her brother's son—like this.

Mushtaq's wife was overcome with grief, as expected. They were a close-knit family and she had watched

Ummer grow up. Meanwhile, her husband was already on the phone, calling for an ambulance first, and then informing the police of the incident. When the ambulance arrived, they climbed in with Ummer. On their reaching the hospital, the doctors confirmed what they already knew. Ummer was dead.

The police wanted to conduct a post-mortem immediately, as it was a part of the procedure in such cases, but Mushtaq asked them to hold off until he could break the news to his brother-in-law and the rest of the family. Till the previous night, the family had been rejoicing as they celebrated Shakeela's niece's wedding. Then, amidst the festivities, Ummer was kidnapped. This had become a common occurrence in the Valley of late and so the family was sure that the kidnappers would return him sooner or later. They had not imagined in their wildest dreams what they were about to hear. Meanwhile, Shakeela and Manzoor, Ummer's paternal uncle, who arrived at the scene almost immediately after Mushtaq had informed him, cleaned the blood off Ummer's body. But while the blood had stopped flowing, their tears would not.

The man lying lifeless on the chowk that day was Lieutenant Ummer Fayaz, a commissioned officer of the Indian Army. He had been shot at close range, twice. One bullet had entered his body through the back, and emerged from his lower abdomen, tearing it apart; the other, hitting the back of the head, had exited from his jaw.

Chapter 1

May 1994

It was the year in which the Indian Parliament had unanimously adopted a resolution emphasizing that Jammu and Kashmir was an integral part of India. The idea was to pressurize Pakistan to vacate parts of the state that it had occupied since 1947. At the same time, the government was charging thirteen Border Security Force (BSF) officers with murder, for allegedly firing into a crowd without provocation, in Kashmir.

Amidst all this and more, Jameela Akhtar was pregnant with her first child. She had married an apple farmer, Fayaz Ahmed Parrey, in 1989. After a long wait of five years, the couple were overjoyed to learn that they had finally conceived. The 'first' is always special in some ways. First love, first house, first bike, first car. The rush of new emotions heightens the happiness.

About a month before the baby was due, Jameela expressed a desire to go to her maternal home, as was the custom in these parts. But Fayaz kept delaying it; he felt only he was capable of looking after her in the best possible way.

One day, she finally confronted him. 'Fayaz, I think it's time for me to pack and leave for my parents' house. It'll be eight months in a few days.'

Fayaz looked up, as if assessing the situation in his mind.

'What do you think?' Jameela quickly asked, determined not to let him find another reason for delaying her journey. There was some frustration in her tone, as her swollen belly and ankles made it impossible for her to be chirpy about anything these days.

Giving in to the inevitable, Fayaz finally sighed and said, 'Okay, when should we go?'

'Tomorrow?' Jameela said, without another thought.

Fayaz only nodded, but Jameela could tell he meant business as he picked up his scooter keys and walked purposefully towards the door. He was a meticulous planner and an endless worrier, so she knew he would plan their little trip to perfection. In the meantime, she decided to put together the things she needed.

Fayaz rode to the nearest market, Yaripora, all geared up for some shopping. His first stop was his favourite bread shop, the one that sold fresh naans.

'*As-salāmu alaykum, bhaijaan!*' The shopkeeper was delighted to see Fayaz.

'*Wa ʿalaykumu as-salām*! How's it going?' Fayaz greeted him in return.

'Everybody eats roti, Fayaz bhai, so I'll never be out of business. Unless, of course, you give up apple farming, and step into this business. Then I will have stiff competition,' he laughed.

Fayaz smiled. He had always been a polite man, loved by the locals for his shy simplicity. 'That will never happen, bhaijaan. I'll stick to my apple farming and orchards. They are my heritage,' he replied.

The shopkeeper nodded and asked softly, 'How is Jameela bhabhi?'

'She's doing well. I am taking her to her mother's, tomorrow. The baby is expected next month. Can I have five naan boxes please?'

The shopkeeper packed the naans for a journey and handed them over to Fayaz. He visited other shops in the market, and every shopkeeper greeted him with the same warmth and familiarity. When he headed back to his scooter, Fayaz was carrying dry fruits, eggs, sugar, a box of sweets and the naans. And a shirt and a pair of trousers for his brother-in-law, Muhammad Maqbool Mir.

Jameela was shocked to see Fayaz walk into the house, loaded with his new purchases.

'Why did you have to go and get so many things?' She asked in exasperation. The very thought of carrying so much on their two-wheeler with her bulging belly was tiring.

'I just wanted to make sure you have tons of nourishing food there every day. Who knows what your parents will feed you there! I don't want my child to be thin and weak, like you and your family. You have to eat well.' Fayaz teased his wife.

Jameela knew her husband well by now, and realized that sarcasm was his way of camouflaging emotions. He wasn't very good at hiding them any more. Not from her. And she knew that he was going to miss her.

* * *

On 9 May 1994, Fayaz and Jameela started for her maternal home, unaware of the tragic significance that date would assume in their future lives. Jameela woke up early and prepared breakfast for her parents-in-law, took a bath and began dressing up for the journey.

'Hurry up, Jameela. Let's leave before it gets too hot and sunny. You won't enjoy that in this state, I'm sure!' Fayaz prodded.

Jameela came out of the bathroom, dried her hair and put on her hijab. She spread her prayer mat on the floor, not too concerned about finding qiblah, the direction of the Kaaba. She had been taught, as a child, that whichever direction she may turn to, she would find Allah.

The morning prayer was a ritual that came naturally to her now, after years of daily practice. Seated on the mat, she raised her hands, bent at the elbows with palms facing in, and began reciting '*Allah-hu-Akbar*'. She then folded her hands across her chest, right over left, in the manner typical of Sunni prayer customs, and recited *Surah Al-Fatihah* along with a few other verses from the Quran. She placed her hands on her knees and bowed to touch her forehead to them. Owing to her pregnancy, the posture made her back ache these days. But she did her best, praising Allah three times in that position. For the final part of her ritual, she sat on the lower part of her legs and offered *sajdah* twice before she concluded her namaz with a *dua* for a healthy baby. Her prayers always ended with the salawat, '*Alayhi as-salam*' (Peace be upon him).

Fayaz waited patiently for her to finish. He had seen Jameela perform prayers diligently all these years, and would never dream of hurrying her through them. But as soon as she was done, he had her bidding farewell to his parents and out of the house. Kick-starting his scooter, he gently helped his wife on to the seat. He had put all her luggage in the front of the scooter where his feet rested, so that she would not be burdened on the ride.

Jameela's parents lived in Batpora, an hour's drive from their house in Kulgam. The road to Batpora wound through fields, some lush with yellow-flowered mustard, some green with paddy, and some radiant with a mix of orchard hues. The apple trees were still blooming, and made them think of the little one who would arrive soon. Fayaz rode gingerly, expertly manoeuvring away from potholes that most motorists would feel all the way through their journey.

'When will the government give us some roads? All I see are potholes,' Fayaz said, shaking his head. With his wife so close to her due date, Fayaz was worried.

Halfway through the ride, they stopped so that Jameela could drink some water. The sun was shining bright upon them, making Jameela uncomfortable. Fayaz had been right; they should have started sooner. Wiping beads of sweat from her forehead and face, Jameela asked Fayaz, 'What do you want? A girl or a boy?'

It was the first time Jameela had brought this up. Fayaz smiled and said, 'It should be a healthy baby. That's all I want.' He paused to look at her, knowing that she'd be living far away from him for many months now. Then he got up abruptly, not wanting to let his emotions get the better of him.

'Come, let's go! I want to be at your house before lunchtime. The baby will be hungry by then.' Knowing this would annoy her, he made sure to hide his smile.

'It's always about the baby and never about me!' Jameela shot back at him, just as he had expected.

They soon reached Jameela's maternal home, where her brother Maqbool lived with their father, Ghulam Rasool Mir, and mother, Zeeba Banu, his wife and three daughters. The house was in Nildang, Batpora, in the Shopian district. It was a small two-storeyed structure with a tin-lined Dutch gable roof. The property was fenced with tin sheets and iron pickets. Jameela and Fayaz walked in, and were greeted with animated warmth by Jameela's parents. They had been waiting to spend quality time with their daughter. Naturally, they were very excited about the baby too.

It was about tea-time and Jameela's brother welcomed them with a lavish spread. There was a lot of love, teasing and banter at the table, as Jameela had come home after a very long time.

Fayaz wanted to start back early as he preferred not to travel after dark. But Maqbool, his brother-in-law, would hear nothing of it. 'Bhaijaan, it's just not safe any more. There are always bullets whizzing through the air, and in the end, we won't even know whose bullet got us. You can leave early in the morning if you like, but not now.'

Fayaz shook his head in frustration, a common sentiment in those days after a recent turn of events in that region. It was simply not safe to be out and about any more—neither during the day, nor at night.

In January 1990, a number of Kashmiri Pandits were murdered or chased out of Kashmir in a so-called ethnic cleansing drive. By 1998, their population had shrunk from an estimated 1,40,000 to a mere 20,000. The Indian Army was eventually deployed to deal with the situation. After all, that kind of violence could only be tackled by power, and power grows out of the barrel of the gun. The Kashmiri Pandits' exodus was not the only cause of unrest. Terrorism and infiltration were at their peak in Kashmir during that time, and had to be contained.

'Boys from every family are picking up guns, Fayaz bhai. Even good, god-fearing families like ours. The situation couldn't be worse,' said Maqbool in a dejected voice.

'Why do you worry, Maqbool? You have such a lovely little girl. Musrat, come here,' Fayaz called out to his niece, patted her head and gave her some candy from his pocket.

Maqbool prepared a bed for Fayaz and asked him to rest. Yet, sleep was distant that night. The situation in Kashmir, exceptionally turbulent of late, was playing on Fayaz's mind and he couldn't help but think about the kind of future he'd be giving his child.

For Jameela, returning to her maternal home was a great relief from the routine responsibilities at her in-laws' house. She rested well, and her family ensured that the unborn child received ample nourishment—of both the mind and the body.

* * *

One day short of a month after Jameela came to her parents, her water broke. Fayaz was summoned and he rushed to Batpora, taking barely half an hour for the ride that had taken about an hour and a half when he had Jameela riding pillion.

On 8 June 1994, Jameela and Fayaz were blessed with a boy. They named him Ummer, commonly pronounced as Umar.

The family got together and Jameela's eldest brother, Nazir Ahmed, recited the *azan* in Ummer's right ear. This was to symbolize that Ummer had been born into the Muslim faith.

'Do you know the meaning of the name "Ummer"?' Fayaz asked Jameela, lifting his son in his arms. Jameela shook her head in the negative.

'It means age. Our boy is going to have a long life.' Fayaz gently rubbed noses with his son, staring in amazement at the little bundle of joy who had come to light up their lives.

'It also means first-born son and an eloquent speaker,' Ummer's maternal grandfather said, proud of his status as a grandparent.

'Yes Abbu, I want my son to be a good orator. He should be able to charm everyone with his speech. I'll teach him everything.'

As soon as he had spoken those words, however, Fayaz's expression turned sad. He realized that, not being very literate himself, he wouldn't be able to contribute much to his son's education. He had failed in the Class X and had not pursued his studies thereafter. But after all, Fayaz consoled himself, he knew how to take care of his apple orchard well, and that was what he did for a living.

The next day, Fayaz's parents visited Batpora. They were overjoyed to finally see their newborn grandson and had got him a set of baby clothes. As was customary, they gifted Rs 500 to the new mother for good luck. Fayaz and his parents then spent a few days at Jameela's home before they returned to Kulgam. It would be a few months before Jameela and Ummer would make their journey back to Kulgam.

One day, Jameela, watching her infant son kick his legs in the air, called out to her father, 'Abbu, I just realized that Ummer is already a month old today.'

Her father said, with the expression of a philosopher, 'No, Jameela. Every life has an end . . . we just don't know when. So Ummer has already lost one month of his life.'

He smiled at Jameela and left for his daily prayers.

Jameela didn't quite understand the depth of her father's words at the time. They were going to become the bitterest truth of her life in the years to come.

Chapter 2

17 May 2017

Eight days after the assassination of Lieutenant Ummer Fayaz

My friend Vishal called, complaining of my lack of empathy for his craving for my mum's mango pickle. I laughed and promised to send some to where he was posted.

Major Vishal Chauhan was then stationed at an army outpost in Kashmir. Vishal has a weakness for my mum's pickles, and has been known to bribe his way into my mum's heart in order to replenish his stash periodically.

As conversations go with friends, one topic led to another and eventually we got down to discussing the Valley. He would be posted in Kashmir for another year at least, Vishal said wryly, and that his life revolved around AK-47s, terrorists, and *Sadbhavana*.

If you are wondering what Sadbhavana is, allow me to digress a little and explain. In the early 1990s, Indian Army units were deployed to combat insurgency in Kashmir. But owing to the way subsequent events unfolded, their presence stirred discontent in the hearts and minds of Kashmiris. In 1998, in an effort to mend relations, the army's Northern Command launched Operation Sadbhavana. It was an effort to extend help in rebuilding the lives of those who had suffered at the hands of terrorists. And that is the army's perspective.

The Kashmiri version of this story is drastically different. They hold the army responsible for all their losses—of lives as well as property. When death claims your dearest ones, anger takes root in the mind and grows like an incurable disease that eventually consumes you. That said, civilian anger and discontentment have also made the army's job in Kashmir much harder.

While some believe the Indian Army has done more damage than good in Kashmir, experts in Delhi insist that, had troops not been deployed in the Valley in the 1990s, Kashmir would no longer be a part of India. While the debate rages on, Kashmir has turned into nothing less than a war zone. Once known for its heavenly beauty, the state is now the stage of a perpetual, grim battle between life and death. The contrast, between the physical beauty of the place and the gory scenes of everyday life, is sometimes stark. This is the land that had once inspired poets and artists, and hosted awed visitors from all over the world. Today, it is synonymous with curfews and deathly silence.

But more than the war on the ground, the army is dealing with war in the minds of the people. They are angry, and the army's very presence is the source of that anger.

I don't think the army has a solution to the conflict in the Valley. They seem to be plugging holes in a bleeding

Kashmir with their bare hands. Noble and heroic as this endeavour may appear, this situation may just need a more sterile approach.

In the 1990s, civil administration more or less collapsed in the Valley, and there was an all-round failure of vital infrastructural support in the fields of education, water supply, medical facilities, roads and transport, to name only a few. There was way too much insurgency for the government to make any substantial progress in terms of civil welfare.

To return to our conversation, Vishal remarked with a hint of disappointment and pain in his voice, 'There was a time when it was simple and could have been solved with ease. Now, it is complex and there are too many fault lines.'

'What do you mean?' I was curious.

'Have you ever tried to detangle headphone wires?' he asked. 'Yes! It's quite frustrating at times.'

'Now think of a situation where you have not one but ten headphones, all entangled. That's the situation in Kashmir now.'

'Tell me more!' I said, ignorant of the political intricacies of the region, like most fellow Indians.

'Can't discuss these sensitive issues over the phone, though. They can, however, be traded for some mango pickle. So, get to work if you want more information.' Vishal knew I was the most inquisitive person on the planet, and was whetting my appetite for his own gain. Ugh!

I pestered him some more, but he changed the topic. 'Did you hear about the Kashmiri officer who was kidnapped and killed?'

It had been on the news, but I couldn't recollect the soldier's name.

'Lieutenant Ummer Fayaz.' Vishal's voice seemed heavy with sorrow.

'The news channels say he was kidnapped from his house. Is that true?' I asked.

'I believe so.'

'You mean you don't know?' I was incredulous, assuming that Vishal was withholding information, yet again, for the mango pickle.

But his tone had become dead serious, 'The investigation is still on.'

'How can you not know what happened to your fellow officer?'

'He wasn't just any fellow officer. He was a Kashmiri. There is a difference. And he didn't die in an army operation. He was kidnapped and murdered.'

I could sense he was struggling with his anger and frustration more than grief, and then I got what I deserved in a burst of annoyance, 'Wait! You didn't even know the name of the officer and you expect me to know the details of a highly sensitive investigation? That's the problem with you guys. It's barely been a week and you have already forgotten his name. And you were the one who forwarded that message to me, about the candlelight march at India Gate in his name. And you forgot his name!'

I winced at his words, all of them true. There are many things we take for granted, and freedom tops the list. In a country like India, surrounded by hostile neighbours, that freedom is bought with the lives of the soldiers who guard it. Dearly bought, for lives are priceless.

'I'm sorry' would have been my normal response. But this time, the words didn't come so easily and I was silent for a fleeting but deeply apologetic moment.

I had indeed forwarded the message about the candlelight march to everybody on my contact list. I had also posted it on my Twitter handle. But it was simply the mandatory forward at the time, one of several causes that touched me—like an emergency alert for a missing child, a call for a kidney donor, or flood relief funds.

A retired colonel of the Indian Army had also messaged me after reading my forwarded message about the candlelight march, asking, 'Why only Lieutenant Ummer Fayaz? Because he was a Kashmiri? So many Indian soldiers are killed in action in that region, almost every other day. Why have we never had a candlelight march for them?'

At the time, it seemed to me that the colonel was making a very sound point. But I had only skimmed the surface, and had no inkling of the depths of the ocean. It was only much later, after diving very deep, that I found the answer to his question, and understood why Lieutenant Ummer Fayaz's death was a travesty of justice, and how it had occurred outside the boundaries of his duty as a soldier of the Indian state.

And Vishal started it all by suggesting, 'You have the power of the pen. Why don't you write a book on him? He was a *fauji*, after all!'

Every single male member of my family has either served in the army or is presently serving in the army. Vishal knew that the fauji sentiment was dear to my heart, and he was asking me to honour it by doing something that I was passionate about. Writing a story.

I was hooked by the idea. A few days later, I was at the office of the Additional Directorate General of Public Information (ADGPI), seeking permission for the book. And it was granted.

I prepared an exhaustive list of people that I wanted to meet in order to get started. Although the writing of the book had been approved by the ADGPI, I had to seek additional permission, as per army protocol, to interview the following people:

- The Rashtriya Rifles (RR) unit, the army unit posted at the location where the incident had occurred
- Lieutenant Ummer Fayaz's family in Kulgam
- His unit (2 Raj Rif)
- His schoolmates and teachers
- His batchmates—juniors and seniors—who had trained with him in the National Defence Academy (NDA) and the Indian Military Academy (IMA)
- The Ustads (instructors) who had trained him in the NDA and the IMA

The sanctioning officer jovially remarked that never in its history of sanctioning books, did the ADGPI have to approve such an exhaustive list.

However, I was insistent and the army was cooperative. Little did they know that the list was only going to get longer.

21 June 2017

Forty-three days after the assassination of Lieutenant Ummer Fayaz

My first stop in Kashmir was Srinagar, where my mother was holidaying with my grandmother and aunts. It was an unscheduled stopover; my flight from Chandigarh to Srinagar was delayed due to bad weather, and I had been advised not to travel in the night. So I had a fun night with the 'girls'. I told them it was research for a new project that had brought me to the Valley, but I was careful not to divulge too many details. I didn't want my folks hitting the panic button before I had even started.

The next morning, my taxi arrived on time. I had made sure to hire an SUV as I am prone to terrible bouts of motion sickness and a sturdy car helps alleviate these somewhat. As I climbed into the vehicle, I recollected that I was missing from the photo-albums of countless family holidays that involved drives. My dread of the motion sickness overwhelming me on these journeys was so great that I often simply refused to go. When I got older, the family would let me drive on most family car trips, with someone else taking over only if I needed a break. And if they braked without warning, more often than not, they'd be covered in vomit the next instant. That's how all the men in the family have become good drivers, my brother quips, adding that a good driver is one who doesn't use the brakes for thousands of kilometres. Of course.

My instructions were to set course for Behi Bagh. I had also been strictly warned not to mention that I was headed for an army camp until I reached Behi Bagh. My initial reticence might have seemed odd to the driver but I decided to follow orders and remained non-committal about where I was headed. The events that unfolded shortly thereafter should be able to explain why.

Srinagar is beautiful but the hour-and-a-half drive to Behi Bagh was so mesmerizing that I forgot to fret over my motion sickness. The green of the plains seemed newly washed by what could only have been heaven-sent showers. The air was incredibly pure. And the apple orchards that lined the roads were burdened with luscious-looking fruit, still green, waiting to turn red in a month or so.

Kashmir is breathtaking. It is hardly surprising that it has captured the imagination of generations of filmmakers and painters, poets and storytellers alike. Yet one cannot help but wonder if the beauty of the land is also its curse, evoking the darker emotions in those who behold it. Of jealousy. And the desire to possess. For over seventy years, India and Pakistan have been locked in conflict over Kashmir. Meanwhile, Kashmiris fight for a future that even they are divided on. Some want *azadi*, some want Islamic government, and a few even want the dispute to last forever simply because it happens to be their bread and butter, but most want peace. In recent years, the crisis has only escalated. It is time the Indian government demonstrated fresh initiative to defuse the situation. Peace is long overdue in the Valley, and the Kashmiri people, after decades of asking for it, are tired. So tired that some have taken up arms against the state.

Kashmir, a blessing that has been ignored for too long, has turned into a curse.

Sleep eluded me, but I was too distracted by the exquisite landscape en route to Behi Bagh, to mind.

The driver didn't seem very chatty, so I initiated the conversation. 'Bhaiya, what is your name?'

'Ahmed Ali.'

'And where are you from?' I pressed on.

'I live in Shopian.'

I had heard that Shopian was a hotbed of terrorism, and almost blurted out a question, asking him why people in his village were picking up guns. But I stopped myself just in time.

'Where are you from?' the driver asked, displaying signs of warming up to the conversation a little. I was pleased.

'I'm from Punjab. Have you heard of the place?'

'Yes, madam. I have, but I have never been there. I have never been outside of Kashmir.'

'You don't have to go, Ahmed bhaiya. Jannat is right here.'

That made Ahmed positively flush with delight. I might just have made a friend, I thought to myself.

'Is this your first visit to Kashmir?' he ventured.

'Yes,' I lied.

I had learnt early in my career as a writer to offer a blank slate to people, especially when information is key to a particular story. By doing so, you allow people to fill it up with their own unique perspective—their version of events.

'Then why are you going to Behi Bagh? You should stay in Srinagar, see the Dal, Nageen and Wular lakes. Ride the Shikara. We have many beautiful gardens . . . Nishat, Chashma Shahi, Shalimar, Pari Mahal. Tourists don't go to Behi Bagh. What will you do there?'

From this barrage of travel recommendations, I could also tell that Ahmed was curious as to why a lone girl would travel to Behi Bagh. He was clearly not impressed with my itinerary.

I had prepped myself to respond with a convincing answer. Although I didn't want to lie to Ahmed, it wasn't a choice at the time. In a place where people had killed their own, I was an outsider. And I understand the subtle difference between bravery and foolishness. Crossing that thin line in a volatile place like Kashmir costs lives.

'I'm a food inspector. I've come to assess the quality of apples in Shopian. If they suit my company's requirements, we will be buying them at a higher price, to use them for juice production.'

I had rehearsed this story about a million times in my mind, and it worked like a charm. Ahmed was delighted and asked if I would inspect his orchards too.

'You have apple orchards?' I asked, hoping he didn't have any questions on what an apple inspector looks for in apples. I happened to be completely clueless about apples, except for knowing that I liked mine crunchy and sweet.

'That's the only means of livelihood in this belt, madam. Apples are our lifeline.'

I couldn't quite gauge if he was happy to tell me that, or sad.

'I'm a graduate, madam. I can speak fluent English. Do you see how I earn a living? Driving a taxi!'

The frustration in his voice was evident now.

'But why? Are there no jobs here?' I asked. I knew there weren't, but my concern was genuine.

'Army! It's the Indian Army that's to blame. The Delhi government never gives us enough. But even if it did, how is it possible for our children to read and write under the shadow of guns?' Ahmed burst out in anger.

'But does the Indian Army trouble you without reason?' As soon as I had uttered these words, there was a loud thud at the back of the car. A BSF jawan had struck the rear of our SUV with his lathi. He was trying to get civilian vehicles to make way for a BSF convoy.

Ahmed braked suddenly, and I threw up. Rolling the window down, Ahmed cursed the BSF jawan.

'Why did you hit my car? I'm keeping to my lane, not breaking any rules. How dare you?' he demanded angrily.

The BSF jawan seemed intent on avoiding a brawl with Ahmed. He quickly returned to his own vehicle, which had a few more jawans, and moved away.

'Did you see, madam, how these people treat us in our own land?' Ahmed was trying to gain my sympathy, but it was I who needed his at that moment, having thrown up all the contents of my stomach. He quickly got me a bottle of water and I rinsed out my mouth as best as I could.

A few metres ahead, we reached a bridge with a river running below it. Remembering that my grandmother had entrusted me with a few sacred threads in Srinagar with instructions to release them in flowing water for good luck, I asked Ahmed to stop.

'Why, madam?'

When I explained, Ahmed seemed a little reluctant to comply. But sensing my resolve, he stopped on the bridge and asked me to hurry. 'If someone sees you doing this, you will be in trouble.'

I completed my ritual and got back in the car.

'Why would I be in trouble?' I asked, a little annoyed at him.

'Religious tolerance is at an all-time low here. People behave irrationally. Sometimes, even when I think I know someone, the things they do . . . it's all so unpredictable these days.'

He must have seen the fear on my face because he was quick to add, 'All people here aren't bad. We care about Kashmiriyat, you see. We take care of our guests, treat them with tolerance . . .'

'What is "Kashmiriyat"?'

I had barely asked the question when Ahmed's phone rang. I couldn't follow what he then said in rapid, chaste Kashmiri, but it was a brief, animated conversation. No sooner had he hung up than he swung the car around, making a complete U-turn. Before I could ask what was happening, a boy appeared in our line of vision, seemingly out of nowhere. He couldn't have been older than sixteen or seventeen; I could see, even before he hurled the stone at our car, that he was puffing his chest to look menacing. The front window of the SUV on the passenger side was hit and the glass smashed. I was surprised at my own reflexes and ducked in time to miss the shards that splattered on to the front and rear seats.

For a few moments, we sat in stunned silence. Then Ahmed accelerated at breakneck speed, taking us far away from the scene. But he kept checking his rear-view mirror to see if I was all right.

'Ahmed bhai, is this the "Kashmiriyat" you were talking about?'

I have this weird impulse to crack jokes in tense situations. A coping mechanism, no doubt. Ahmed grinned, looking very embarrassed. Meanwhile, I was silently thanking god that I had survived this incident with zero injuries. But clearly, Ahmed's explanation of 'Kashmiriyat' would have to wait for another time.

'What now, Ahmed bhai?' I asked, my heart still racing with stark fear.

'Madam, there is stone-pelting at Pampore. We drivers watch out for each other . . . that was a friend who had called to caution me. The safest place for you right now is an army camp. There is one near Pampore. Once the situation improves, we can go ahead.'

Ahmed made another call, speaking in Kashmiri again, so I had no clue what this conversation was about either. We reached an army camp that I recognized instantly from the barricades and the uniforms of the armed guards who stopped us at the gate to ID us.

Ahmed explained the situation to them. He deposited his licence at the gate and entered details of the vehicle in a register.

Once in the familiar environs of an army camp, a semblance of calm returned to me. Soon, I was seated at a table on the lawns. My throat felt parched, and as if on cue, I was served some water. It was swiftly followed by tea with biscuits. Having made sure I was comfortable, Ahmed had gone over to speak to some soldiers who seemed to know him well.

Just as I was finishing my tea, I was offered lunch. Truth be told, I was famished, especially after the contents of my stomach had been hurled out so violently earlier in the day. But I didn't want to eat if we didn't have the time. I looked over at Ahmed in the distance, apparently deep in discussion with one of the soldiers. He then walked abruptly towards me with the soldier.

'Madam, you should eat lunch here. The locals haven't settled down as yet.'

My curious and observant mind registered the interesting fact that Ahmed had not referred to them as miscreants or stone-pelters.

'What about you, Ahmed?' I asked, concerned.

'I'll be fine, madam. I'm carrying my lunch with me.' Evidently, he did not wish to have lunch at the camp.

'Why are the locals pelting stones?' I asked, determined to get some answers.

Ahmed and the soldier exchanged looks, each waiting for the other to speak. When Ahmed didn't show any sign of wanting to talk, the soldier finally said, 'Madamji, there was an encounter yesterday and we killed three terrorists. Three weapons were also recovered. It was in the news. Didn't you see?'

From his accent, I could make out that the jawan was from Garhwal. 'So this stone-pelting is an act of protest? Why would locals protest over the killing of a terrorist?' I was puzzled.

'That is how it plays out here.' The jawan smiled as he placed my teacup on the tray he was carrying.

'Lunch is ready, madam.'

Hunger is a great appetizer, and there are few meals I've relished in my life as much as I did the lunch that followed.

Ahmed brought the car around for us to leave. As soon as we were on our way, I resumed my earlier line of inquiry, for there were several niggling questions on my mind.

'Why did you take me to the camp, Ahmed bhai?'

'For your safety, madam.'

'So the army does protect you?'

'Why must they protect me from my own people? They are the ones who murder and then we have to pay the price for it.' His voice was calm but the bitterness and frustration were hard to miss.

'How?'

'They kill innocent people who only want what's good for us. This protest was for our people. Do you know the frustration one faces when some of your own get killed and you can't do anything about it?'

Fortunately, I hadn't experienced that in my life, and thanked god for that. But I pressed on, 'Innocent people who carry guns?'

'Doesn't the army use guns on us? If an angry, frustrated man picks up a gun in retaliation, why does it surprise the world?'

'He can study, get a job and make something of his life. Help people around him. Let development take place rather than blow up an institution that provides jobs to its own people.' I reasoned, reminded of the blasts that took place in the Entrepreneurship Development Institute (EDI) buildings twice. We lost a few soldiers, of whom, Captain Pawan Kumar and Captain Tushar Mahajan were very young.

'Oh sure. Like no one has tried that before. A perfect example is right in front of you, madam. I have a degree in civil engineering, but I toil in my apple orchard and drive a taxi.'

There was a long, pregnant silence in the car for a while after that. I wanted to tell him that there was a difference between legitimate and illegitimate power. That the means are as important as the end in any struggle, and that a constitutional state cannot be made or unmade by the unconstitutional machinery of terrorism. I wanted to tell him that he was naïve and foolish to think that terrorism was the solution to his problems. But I didn't say anything at all, because I felt I simply didn't know enough about the place or its people to have earned the right to an opinion. Not yet. Besides, sometimes the story from another perspective seems equally plausible. And also, to be honest, I wasn't too keen on provoking him, not after seeing him get angry at the BSF jawan on the road earlier.

The sun was about to set when we approached Behi Bagh. Ahmed now wanted to know exactly where to drop me off.

'At the army camp, Ahmed bhai.' He didn't seem in the least surprised.

We were stopped at the gates of 62 RR and repeated the drill, as per army protocol, of depositing Ahmed's licence and making an entry in the register. This time, they asked me to deposit my ID cards too. But I knew they were in safe hands. These soldiers keep a country of 1.3 billion Indians safe every day, I told myself.

There were no hotels near Lieutenant Ummer's home, and even if there had been any, they wouldn't have been safe options to choose from. So I had requested accommodation at the army camp that was closest to

his house. The commanding officer, also known as the CO
or Tiger, had been informed of my arrival well in advance.
He knew who I was and the purpose of my visit to Shopian,
and had received an instructional code to be followed
during my stay.

'Welcome to Jannat, ma'am.' The CO, Colonel Manu
Sudan, greeted me with warm cordiality.

He continued, gesturing at the vast expanse around
us, 'Undoubtedly, this is paradise on earth. But like in the
Biblical story, when God creates paradise, he also slips in a
snake to test human resolve.'

I wasn't sure I agreed with that. 'It's not the doing of the
gods, the destruction of this beautiful place; it's ours. And in
man's fight for land, human lives are being compromised.'

He merely smiled at that, and then came briskly to the
point, 'You're writing a book on Lieutenant Ummer Fayaz?'

I nodded in affirmation. The CO's expression all
through this conversation remained neutral, making it
difficult for me to gauge his sentiments.

'So, what is your plan of action?' he inquired.

I knew I had to visit Lieutenant Ummer's parents'
house the next day. It was something that one can never
quite prepare for—a condolence visit to a family that had
just lost a loved one. To death so sudden, so brutal and
so untimely.

I made my intentions clear to the CO. He then wanted
to know about my plans after the visit.

'I would like to visit the school he went to. I believe it's
run by the army?'

'The central government runs the school; the army only
protects it. The school is in Anantnag, and another RR

unit is placed there. But we can organize that visit for you. Can I catch up with you later today? Our unit is hosting an iftar party for local Muslims. And I have to make sure everything is in perfect order. If you're awake, please do join us for a late dinner. You may like the delicacies from the iftar menu. Or if you prefer to dine in, Shubh Karan has been deputed to take care of you while you are with us. Just let him know.'

Impeccable manners. His unit was hosting an iftar meal that evening, and he had come around just to make sure I felt welcome. At the same time, I wondered why a school would need military protection.

Remember the strict army protocol I'd mentioned, of taking permission for every bit of research related to the book? Well, Colonel Manu was the only officer in this unit whom I was allowed to interview. But Colonel Manu was the senior-most officer, if it was any consolation, commanding nearly 1200 heavily armed troops.

I sat on the small lawn outside my room, which offered an impressive view of the picture-perfect landscape surrounding the camp. But my thoughts were now occupied with the impending visit to Lieutenant Ummer's home. How could I offer my condolences? Could my words provide even a semblance of solace to a family that had so recently lost their beloved son? My sombre mood was not exactly conducive to socializing, and I told Shubh Karan that I would prefer to eat in. I didn't know then that this meeting which I was already so anxious about, would be a gut-wrenchingly emotional experience for me too.

As night approached, sleep eluded me. Anxiety was mounting. After tossing and turning in bed for a while,

I began channel-surfing in a last-ditch effort to calm my nerves. There was no mobile network in my room, or I could have taken refuge in YouTube. Instead, television channels bombarded me with news that did nothing to lift my mood. 'DSP Ayub Pandith lynched to death,' shouted one news anchor. 'The Valley has turned barbaric,' declared another.

The Valley had done nothing. No! It was some people who had turned barbaric, I felt. A place is nothing without its people, and when they go awry, the land itself bears the brunt. These disturbing reports from the Valley further weakened my morale that night.

I was glad when morning came and Shubh Karan knocked at my door to ask what I would like for breakfast. Knowing I had a long day ahead of me, I asked for an omelette, two slices of bread and some coffee.

Breakfast done, I was all set for the day. Shubh Karan appeared right on cue to say that my vehicle was ready, and that Colonel Manu would like to speak to me before I left. Shubh Karan took me to the CO's office. A junior commissioned officer (JCO) opened the door and let me in. The walls of the room were painted a soft cream colour, creating an atmosphere that was in complete contrast with the grim expression on Colonel Manu's face. His eyes were glued to a news channel on TV as he signed his way through a heap of documents.

'Ma'am, a DSP has been killed in Srinagar.' I knew that the CO was talking about Muhammad Ayub Pandith. An ironic name for a man in the Valley, I thought. At the gate of Jamia Masjid on the night of Shab-e-Qadr, when forgiveness for sins is earned by prayer, a man with

Muhammad and Pandith in his name had been murdered for performing his duty.

'Ma'am, we are on red alert and the area is volatile. I'm sending a local escort, Iqbal, with you. He knows the place and the family. Try to keep your visit down to fifteen minutes. And always, use your instincts. If you notice anything suspicious, call us immediately.'

Colonel Manu's instructions were crisp and clear. I knew the situation was serious and that I was in a place where taking a risk could put an end to my life. I put the three phone numbers he gave me on speed dial, then took his leave and followed Shubh Karan to the vehicle that had been assigned to me. I was carrying only a small bag with bare essentials for a short trip. Shubh Karan introduced me to Iqbal and bid us goodbye. Once we set off, I asked my escort by way of breaking the ice, 'Iqbal bhaiya, is what I'm wearing all right for the visit?'

I was wearing a churidar, and had draped a dupatta over my head, in an attempt to dress modestly for the occasion, aware of the fact that most people judge by appearance. It was important for me to look like one of them for better acceptance.

'Yes madam, but don't worry about it. People are not so narrow-minded here,' Iqbal said with a slight smile. I noticed that the driver threw him a disgusted glance.

'How long will we take to reach?'

'We are just ten minutes away, madam.'

My heart started pounding loudly and I could feel it thump away in my chest, and I was sure they could hear it too.

'Do you know the family, Iqbal bhaiya?' My voice quivered a little.

'Yes madam! Very well indeed. We are almost neighbours.'

'Did you know Lieutenant Ummer?' I asked, my tone softer than I had intended it to be.

'Yes madam! I did.'

He said no more and I fell silent. Honestly, I was an emotional wreck myself at that moment, and hoped against hope that the tears wouldn't start until I got back to the army camp.

Chapter 3

I was jolted out of my reverie when the car stopped in front of a small gate. Iqbal told me this was Lieutenant Ummer's house. I braced myself for the moment I had been dreading.

'Madam, please wait while I go inside and have a word with them. I will come and get you in a few minutes,' Iqbal said, briskly getting out of the vehicle.

'So you're writing a book on Ummer Fayaz?' the driver inquired. I looked at him, surprised. 'How do you know?'

'It's a small village, madam. News here travels faster than you can imagine, especially through the apple orchards.'

There's a saying in Punjabi that roughly translates to, 'When the villages are small, mouths are big.' I didn't want to be a victim of rumours in this village, where a young man had recently been killed because of the way some people had perceived him.

'Madam, please come in,' Iqbal called out.

I walked slowly and deliberately to the gate. A couple stood there, waiting to receive me. Iqbal introduced them as Lieutenant Ummer's uncle and aunt. Their manner was cordial, but I could see that they were grief-stricken and not quite sure of me.

They led me up three flights of stairs and through a narrow corridor connecting the third-floor landing to a big carpeted room. There was no furniture; I assumed it must have been cleared out after Lieutenant Ummer's demise so the family could receive visitors who came to offer condolences. It was only later that I learnt that Kashmiris prefer to sit on the floor in their homes.

The entire family was seated on the floor. I found a corner next to the ladies and Iqbal sat some distance away, with the men. This was a practice I had observed in condolence visits in my own city too. And now, at this crucial moment, I did not want to take any chances.

The haggard faces and sad demeanour of my hosts intensified the atmosphere of gloom in the house as well as the heaviness in my heart. The family had borne a loss, but the nation too had lost a brave son. And I was part of that nation. It would be inhuman to not feel the loss as my own. When I look back now, I realize that a part of me must also have identified with the grief of losing a brother and I imagined my parents in a similar situation. That is the only way I can explain why I reacted the way I did that day.

The family now looked at me with curiosity. Suddenly, I was unable to speak, choking on my tears and trying to fight them with all my might. And when I couldn't endure it any longer, the tears just flowed copiously, from unsuspected depths of sorrow in my heart. Though the family's loss had been immense, one that could perhaps never be adequately mourned, their tears stopped for a brief moment and they all came up to me, consoling me as if I were one of their own. I learnt in that moment that few things can bring people together like grief and loss can. In the shared pain of Lieutenant Ummer's death, a new bond was forged between the bereaved and the outsider. And I was allowed to cry. Amidst the many relatives and acquaintances gathered there that day, I somehow managed to connect with the family at the deepest level.

When my tears had abated a little, Iqbal spoke to the family in Kashmiri. Knowing we didn't have much time to complete the task at hand, he explained to me that he had just informed them I was an author from Bengaluru who had come to interview them.

'No Iqbal, let them know that today I won't interview them. I just can't. Today, I am here only to pay my condolences and respect to the family of a brave soldier,' I spoke through my tears.

Ummer's sister, Asmat, gestured to me to come sit next to her, and began talking to me.

'Why have you come so far? Did you know Ummer?' she asked gently.

I answered softly, and honestly, 'No, I didn't know Lieutenant Ummer. I'd never met him. I've come here to ask you about Ummer so that I can write a book about him. I am a writer by profession, and I want the world to know about the brave soldier your brother was.'

I had googled the family before I went to meet them. I knew Ummer was survived by two siblings, both sisters. Unfortunately, the younger sister was in school that day and I couldn't meet her.

'Your brother was a brave soul,' I mustered the strength to say.

'Now we have forgotten what being brave means. Or happiness, for that matter. I don't know if we will ever come out of the darkness of Ummer's death.'

As soon as she said this, I started crying again. Asmat changed the topic to distract me. 'Who do you call family?'

'There's my mother, my father and a brother who is now married.'

'What does your brother do?' she asked. I looked her in the eye but could not gather the courage to answer. I was torn with pain over the shared experience of being sister to a brother in the army. I could relate to the agony, love and loss—every emotion that Asmat was going through. Even today, thinking about that question gives me goosebumps.

We spent a few more minutes with the family and then Iqbal gestured to me that it was time to leave. Although I hadn't interviewed them that day, I felt I already had answers to some questions that hadn't and needn't be asked. I took their leave and made my way to the gate with Iqbal leading the way. Asmat wanted to come out with me, but I asked her to stay back. Once back inside the vehicle, though my heart was still heavy from my emotional encounter, I couldn't help thinking about how pretty all the girls I had seen were. The five-year-old who had walked in just when I was leaving was perhaps the prettiest little girl I have ever seen in my life.

The ride back to the camp was sombre. My mood was such that nothing seemed to catch my eye or attention on the way. I suddenly realized I needed some cash and asked my escort, 'Iqbal, is there an ATM nearby? I need to withdraw some money.'

'Yes, we have one just outside the camp. In any other, you may not find cash.'

'Why is that?' I was a little surprised. After all, ATMs are a basic convenience these days.

Iqbal smiled a strange smile. 'The terrorists make off with entire ATM machines in these parts. The only working machine in this area is the one near the camp. CO Sir's madam got it installed,' he said, referring to Colonel Manu's wife.

This certainly wasn't the first time I'd heard of an ATM robbery. But the mention of miscreants carrying away entire machines, with the result that not a single functioning ATM existed in the area besides the one secured by the army, spoke volumes about the law and order situation there. I wondered how the CO's wife had got one installed though, and asked Iqbal about it.

'She works in a bank in Delhi,' he said with considerable pride. I could tell, however, that the actual source of his pride was his 'CO Saab', and 'madam' was merely an accessory to this tale.

* * *

At the ATM, I recollected Iqbal's stories and deliberated whether to withdraw only the amount I would need for the time being, or stock up on cash in case the machine got robbed. But then it occurred to me that in a hypothetical situation, at gunpoint, with my life in peril, money would hardly matter! So I withdrew a small sum.

On reaching the camp, I went straight to my room and crashed into a deep sleep. It was evening when I woke again, to the sound of Colonel Manu's voice just outside, addressing his troops. I walked up to him, and when he noticed me, he ordered the troops to disperse.

'Is there some place I can go for a run outside camp?' I asked casually. Colonel Manu looked at me as though I had just asked for an Olympic-sized heated indoor swimming pool. I realized, belatedly, that going out alone was not even a remote possibility and that I must have sounded insane to him. I could already almost visualize Shubh Karan or Iqbal having to escort me on a morning run. Indians who don't live in a volatile zone like Kashmir are simply not wired to think like that. Our freedom, to go for a run or to the market or to a friend's place on the spur of the moment, is so taken for granted, we hardly think of it as a conscious act that would need so much forethought.

In fact, with so many responsibilities on his shoulders already, I am sure Colonel Manu wanted me out of his hair and his patch as quickly as possible. As if the situation with the locals and terrorists was not enough, here I was, an added liability in his repertoire.

Colonel Manu said, 'Ma'am, for as long as you are in our camp, you will not step out unless you have explicit permission and a designated escort.' I heard the command in his voice loud and clear, and nodded like a child who had just been scolded for a silly request.

Then with a softer expression, he added, 'Do join us for dinner. Just make sure to stay safe while you go about your business.' He smiled and I smiled back, feeling quite my chirpy self again.

'And as for running,' the Colonel said, 'we have a makeshift gym of sorts. If you would like to use the facility, Shubh Karan can assist you. Just don't expect much from it. We can discuss other matters over dinner.' That was a polite 'over and out' for me, so I took my leave. Burning calories usually helps me expunge persistent, disturbing thoughts and feelings. So I headed to the gym, to work out the rigours of the day. Having thrown my worries out with the sweat, I came back to the room to get dressed for dinner. In fact, since it was already quite cold and there was no geyser facility available, I had to forgo the shower and content myself with a change of clothes.

I found Colonel Manu sitting with a few of his unit officers on a small patch of a lawn outside his humble dwelling. Some of the officers were on their mobile phones while the others were talking to each other. As I approached, all of them fell silent at once; even the phone conversations ended abruptly. Was this an instance of army etiquette, some part of the impeccable code of conduct among officers that I had completely missed in the past? I wondered.

It soon dawned on me that the actual reason was that they didn't want to discuss official matters in my presence. The peril of an information leak is ever present, even within military units, and I was an outsider.

'Good evening, ma'am. Welcome to camp.' All the officers greeted me and then introduced themselves by their first names. Among them was a medical doctor from Kerala, Joseph.

'So, ma'am, how was your day?' Colonel Manu asked after offering me a chair.

I briefed him on the events of the day. He was a patient and attentive listener, a trait that I have found to be common among people who hold responsible positions.

'So they didn't tell you who killed him?' Colonel Manu asked. It was evident that he now wanted some information out of me.

'I couldn't talk much because it was the first time I was meeting them. Plus, you had instructed me to come back early,' I lied. In truth, I had chosen not to interview the family that day.

'Now what?' the CO asked.

'I would like to go back again tomorrow.'

He didn't say anything to that, just offered me a plate from the table, saying, 'You must be hungry. Why don't we get you some dinner?'

I served myself some food and the rest of the officers followed suit.

Colonel Manu lit a cigarette instead.

'Hope you don't mind my smoking,' he said courteously.

'As a matter of fact, I do,' I said in a serious tone, and added with a smile, 'but if you let me go to Lieutenant Ummer's house again, I promise not to take offence.'

He smiled at me, took a drag from his cigarette and seemed to measure his words before saying, 'Ma'am, you don't understand. The family couldn't protect their own son from their own people. How will they protect you? And if something happens to you, I will be held responsible. Even if a *matka* (pot) breaks in a local house, they hold the army responsible. I request you to avoid going tomorrow. This place isn't safe.'

There was nothing I could say to that. He was only trying to protect me in a territory he knew much better than I did. And, after all, he was in charge. The rest of the dinner passed in relative silence until a jawan came over to our table and spoke to Colonel Manu in hushed tones.

The CO leapt out of his chair, saying, 'Sorry ma'am, duty calls. I have to get to my office right now.'

'Hope everything is fine!' I called after him, not knowing what urgent communication had galvanized the Colonel into action during his restful dinner hour.

'When the rest of the world is saying, "Thank god it's Friday", we're saying, "Oh god, it's Friday". Welcome to the jungle, ma'am,' he shot back before he strode off.

I yelled, 'Colonel Manu, I'm not leaving until I get my work done. So if you don't let me visit the family, you will unwillingly be hosting me for a long, long time.' I managed to complete the sentence before he was out of earshot.

I knew this was a bad proposal for the CO. The last thing he would want was to be responsible for my safety for an extended period of time.

He stopped midway, turned and said, 'I'll see what can be done tomorrow. You have a good night's sleep. If you hear any alarms go off, just get under the bed.'

I suddenly did not feel as cocky as I had sounded earlier. What alarms?! Why alarms?!

Shubh Karan walked me to my room, as the electric lights in the camp had been turned off after dark, as per army protocol. The first thing that I looked at when I stepped into my room was the bed. It was impossible for me to crawl under it as its sides touched the floor!

'Bhaiya, if they sound an alarm, how do I get under the bed?' I asked Shubh Karan.

He inspected the bed and said, 'Ma'am, get under anything, perhaps this table.' He pointed at the study table with a lopsided smile on his face. It was evident that my anxiety amused him not a little.

'By the way, why would the alarms go off? What was the CO talking about?' I asked, dreading the answer.

'Ma'am, army camps are always top targets for terrorist groups. If the camp is attacked, an alarm goes off. As armed soldiers, we take our positions. Any unarmed person in the camp is asked to take cover. We also have drills to prepare for the same,' Shubh Karan explained casually as I felt myself turn pale with fear.

'Has an attack ever happened here before?' My voice trembled. 'Not till date, ma'am, but we stay prepared.' He smiled.

How cheerful he sounds, I thought, as he left the room. I didn't know how I would react to an alarm if one were to go off that night, but I knew one thing for sure . . . the resolve of these soldiers was something to be proud of.

* * *

The next day, I was woken up by a phone call. It was Colonel Manu. 'Ma'am, your vehicle should be ready in half an hour. Please finish your work as early as possible.'

I couldn't believe my luck. This was splendid news! I leapt out of bed and was ready in a few minutes.

Less than an hour after the CO's phone call, I was at Lieutenant Ummer's home once again. This time, Asmat and her aunt took me to a different room upstairs. By now, they knew I was a well-wisher and seemed to trust me a little more. Once seated on the carpeted floor, I took out my recorder.

'Hope you don't mind me recording our conversation?' I asked Asmat politely. 'It's to make sure I remember everything.'

'It's okay,' she said. 'But tell me, why are you writing a book on Ummer?'

'Memory is selective and temporary. So much happens in this country each day and often people barely take a day to forget and move on. But can you ever forget this? No! Consider this my attempt to immortalize his story in words. I want his life to be an inspiration for the youth of Kashmir and our nation.'

She seemed to understand. Just then, the little girl I'd seen the previous day entered the room. I called out to her but she was too shy to come to me. I pulled a bar of chocolate out of my bag and tried to lure her with it. She slowly inched closer and Asmat made her sit on her lap.

'What's your name?' I asked, handing her the chocolate and noticing that she had blue eyes.

'Aaeena Mazaffar,' she answered in a low voice.

'How old are you, Aaeena?'

'Five.' She looked down at the chocolate, and then asked me, 'Can you get my Sahibji back?' Realizing she was referring to Ummer, I shed a tear at her innocence and my helplessness.

'Bhaiya used to play with her and get her chocolates. We told her that you're writing a book about him. Maybe she still believes that someone can bring her Sahibji back,' Asmat's voice cracked with pain, and I couldn't restrain my tears either.

That day, I asked many questions, most of which were answered. Asmat told me how Ummer had been kidnapped and how his bullet-ridden body was found the next day. It was hard just to listen to this; I can only imagine what the family must have gone through.

'Do you know who killed him?' It was my final question for Asmat.

She didn't say anything. I could sense that her silence was the reflection of a deep-rooted fear. The terrorists seemed to have accomplished their mission, which was clearly larger and more sinister than even the killing of Lieutenant Ummer Fayaz. It was to sow fear in the hearts and minds of the locals, and it was evident that they had succeeded.

I bade the family farewell, not knowing when or if I would ever get to see them again.

* * *

After reaching the camp that day, I couldn't eat a morsel. To make matters worse, I threw up repeatedly. Shubh Karan came around twice at lunchtime, to accompany me to the mess. He came again at teatime but I just wasn't up to it. Asmat's voice kept playing in my head, especially her description of how they had found Lieutenant Ummer's body.

When Shubh Karan knocked at dinner-time, I was hunched over the sink in the bathroom, emptying the contents of my stomach for the umpteenth time. He had come to give me a message from Colonel Manu; the CO was insisting that Dr Joseph give me a thorough examination. I agreed, hoping he would prescribe some medicine that would help remove the sour taste in my mouth, although the sourness in my heart was probably here to stay.

'How many times have you thrown up?' asked Dr Joseph.

'Eight times,' I replied, my voice hoarse from all the involuntary regurgitation.

'The CO did warn you that none of this is for the faint-hearted,' he said, shrugging his shoulders.

I did not want to talk about it. 'Now what?' I asked instead. I'd grown so weak that I could hardly walk, and my stomach felt so hollow that it seemed to touch my backbone.

'We'll have to put you on drips. Can you walk to the medical room?'

I really didn't want to leave the comfort of my room, so I asked if he could give me the medication there instead.

'Okay, lie down.'

I obeyed, and Dr Joseph asked Shubh Karan to get the medicines and injections he would need from the medical room.

'Let's hydrate you first and then we'll see about our next course of action.'

He looked for a vein on my right arm, but couldn't find one. Locating one in my left arm didn't prove any easier, presumably because the incessant vomiting had drained my body of its electrolytes.

'Your veins are very thin,' Joseph said, more to himself than to me, I thought. In any case, he was telling me something that I already knew. He finally looked up with a smile and said, 'For most of my patients, I could throw a needle from a distance and it would still hit a vein.'

I managed a weak laugh that took the last vestiges of my energy, but could not restrain my inquisitiveness.

'Whom do you treat here?'

'The locals, ma'am. Medical aid is a part of Sadbhavana. Several Public Health Centres (PHCs) set up by the state government don't even have doctors, as many are unwilling to work in the Valley. So the army steps in. I've performed all sorts of medical procedures . . . from delivering babies to surgeries on gunshot wounds.'

'You're a one-man show then! Must be a lot of work if you're the only doctor in the area?'

I couldn't imagine one man taking care of so many people single-handedly.

'Too many people here are willing to kill and injure. I'm probably one of the few in the Valley who heal,' he said with justifiable pride.

'Then you're a very valuable resource, I must say.' Joseph smiled at that.

'When Lieutenant Ummer was killed, some channels telecast the news without doing their research. So they ended up telling the whole world that an army doctor from Shopian had been killed. I'm the only doctor here. You can imagine the anxiety of my family and friends. I must have got no less than a hundred phone calls that day.'

Despite his smile, I knew that day must have been tough to handle. 'The media can sometimes be utterly irresponsible. Especially when it comes to reporting deaths,' I concurred.

'The consequences could be disastrous. My father is a heart patient, ma'am. Imagine how something like this could affect him.'

He was visibly disturbed now, and seemed to want to change the topic. 'So, how was your visit to the family today?'

'Painful and exhilarating at the same time.'

'Well, I can see that. Hope the family was cooperative.'

'Yes, they spoke very freely to me. Why do you ask?'

'Because many reporters went to their place, and they didn't talk.'

'How do you know this?'

Joseph smiled as he replied, 'Everything goes through CO Sir and the unit here, ma'am. And we look after everyone who goes through us. In fact, today, before you entered Lieutenant Ummer's house, CO Sir had ensured that the place was cordoned off. No one was allowed to enter or come out of the house while you were there. Here we trust everyone, but we have no choice but to suspect everyone too.'

I finally understood why everyone in camp maintained silence around me.

'Really? Is the situation that bad?'

'There are over fifty terrorists, armed with AK-47s, on the loose in this area alone. Some of their attacks don't even get covered by the media. And it doesn't help that this is a small village perched on very difficult terrain.'

It was a shocking revelation that a simple visit like mine had entailed so many security measures. I was still struggling to digest the information when Shubh Karan came in with the medicines and the IV. Joseph tried inserting a needle in three different veins before hitting one. He was just about to leave the room when we heard shots fired in the camp. I looked at him in utter panic, wondering what to expect now.

He came back, smiling, and explained as he adjusted my IV bottle, 'Don't worry, ma'am. This sounds like a drill. It's also to convey the message that we are alert and ready. If the firing doesn't stop though, you need to run. Make sure you carry the IV bottle in your hand and run as fast and as far as you can.'

I could never make out when these men were being serious and when they were joking. In fact, they seemed to be living on the edge all the time, where everything was a serious joke. I guess when you put your life at risk every day, that sort of humour is needed to survive.

Before leaving, Joseph instructed Shubh Karan to watch the IV bottle and call him when it was empty. He reckoned that this would take about an hour. Exhausted, I fell asleep for a bit while Shubh Karan sat right outside my room. But it turned out that he somehow missed calling Dr Joseph at the right time. When the doctor returned, he wasn't pleased that the bottle was already empty.

He instructed Shubh Karan to get him another IV bottle and to also open the room next door. He said that he would rest there, as he wanted to make sure there were no more hiccoughs.

'The air shouldn't enter your veins,' he said.

'I'm hallucinating, doctor, I think I'm stressed,' I managed to say.

'Only natural, given the events of yesterday and today. Rest. I'll give you an anti-anxiety pill. That will help.'

It must have, because I slept through the rest of that night.

Joseph later told me that five bottles of IV were administered to me through the night. The morning had me feeling much better, though not my best.

'Hope you're feeling good, ma'am!' Joseph said, coming in. I nodded with a smile.

'Sorry to have kept you awake the whole night,' I said, pulling out a chair for him.

'Just doing my duty, ma'am, and I'm glad you're feeling better. I just came to check on you. Now I'll go and catch up on some sleep in my room.'

Shubh Karan brought my breakfast tray, and a message that Colonel Manu wanted to see me.

'Ma'am, I hear we got you sick?' The CO smiled as he gestured to me to take a seat.

'No, not at all. It's just been an emotional roller coaster. But I don't want you thinking that I'm not brave enough to handle this project.'

It was probably a lame move on my part, trying to sell my bravery to a person whose name was on the hit list of every terrorist in town.

Colonel Manu smiled again and said, 'I'm not judging you, ma'am, and tears aren't always a sign of weakness. I too have had my share. I'm sure you're doing your job well, but I wanted to meet you in person to let you know that Lieutenant Ummer's childhood school is closed for Eid and will reopen only after fifteen days.'

I was deeply disappointed and it must have shown on my face. But there was not much I could do under the circumstances, except for taking a temporary step back.

'I'll come back then, Colonel.'

'You're most welcome, ma'am. But just out of curiosity, how and where is your book going to end?'

'Where do you think it should end, Colonel Manu?' I shot back.

'I think your book would be incomplete until those responsible for Lieutenant Ummer's death are brought to book.'

'Then I'll wait eagerly for you to offer me closure on the book, Colonel.'

When I said that, little did I know of the many twists and turns that the narrative of my book would take before it ended.

Chapter 4

A day later, I was packed and ready to leave for home. Ahmed bhai was hired again to take me to the airport. I bade goodbye to everyone at the camp who had taken such good care of me, including Shubh Karan, and took some pictures as souvenirs of my time there.

My mother, grandmother and aunts were still in Kashmir, and I wanted to meet them before I left. After a short journey through the picturesque route we'd taken only a few days earlier, I arrived at their dwelling in the beautiful city of Srinagar.

Naïvely, I had expected them to be thrilled by my surprise visit. On the contrary, I was met with eerie stone-cold silence. This was a room full of women whom I have known to be exceptionally happy, warm and loud when together. For a moment I panicked, my heart skipping a beat as I imagined all sorts of bad news that they were perhaps about to break to me. But then I have a trained nose for the maternal side of the family, and soon realized that something else was cooking. Maybe, I thought, this was a prelude to some tactical manoeuvre to make me meet some 'nice' boy they wanted me to consider marrying.

I was offered an elaborate high tea, and yet at the table, there was no conversation about me at all. They are all wonderful cooks, and I savoured the home-made goodies while still regarding them with suspicion. Were they fattening me up for the altar, like a sacrificial lamb?

And then the High Priestess, my mother, spoke in chilly tones, 'You are writing a book on a Lieutenant Ummer Fayaz, we heard.'

So this was about that?! How on earth did my mother know? Someone must have called to warn her of my latest adventure. I simply nodded, the best I could do given the circumstances.

'Isn't he the officer who was recently killed by terrorists in the Valley?'

So she had all the information already. My throat had gone dry, as if I was under interrogation for committing some heinous crime. I took a slow sip of my tea to buy time.

'You are not writing any book!' My mother's diktat had the familiar tone of finality. And it seemed to encourage the others to air their opinions.

'Have you gone totally mad?' my aunt shrilled. Even though it was deceptively framed as a question, I knew that if I answered, she would get mad.

Predictably, my grandmother's words were the most dramatic: 'I might as well allow you to jump in a lake full of crocodiles.'

Not one of them was reticent about airing their opinion on my new venture. I don't think we've had any shy people in our family for at least four generations now. Must be missing from our gene pool.

As always, my mother delivered the final lines, a closing argument that seemed to clinch the case for good. Having lived the better part of her life in an 'army' family, she had an intuitive and astute understanding of the dangers that could befall me on this project.

'You will be writing pro-army and against the terrorists who killed Lieutenant Ummer. Do you expect them to let you get away with that? I don't want to lose my child to this mindlessness.'

I had learnt growing up that the best way to kill an argument was to agree. Besides, I had more questions than answers at this point. And I did *not* want to miss my flight, just a few hours away. Because I was flying away from a place they thought could kill me, my family sped me on my way. I could sense the tension and the love in their goodbyes, but a girl's got to do what a girl's got to do. I bade them a hasty farewell and hopped into a cab. I had been told at the camp to check in early for the flight as the security procedures would take time. It was only when I reached the airport that I understood what they meant.

The security procedures at Srinagar airport were unbelievable. It all started with me showing them my ticket at the airport's entrance gate. A few metres ahead of the gate, the vehicle was thoroughly checked by CRPF jawans. 'For weapons or any suspicious items,' they explained to me. All my baggage then passed through an electronic scanner, and I was frisked with a hand-held metal detector. I finally made it to the airport's main gate. All this before even entering the airport premises, and several metres away from the main building!

'*Khuda hafiz*, Ahmed bhai,' I said, handing over the fare money and a tip to him. I had bid him farewell, uttering traditional words that meant 'May God protect you.'

'*Allah hafiz*, madam,' Ahmed replied. It meant, 'May Allah protect you.'

I didn't know if Allah and Khuda had different meanings for Ahmed but nevertheless I smiled back at Ahmed as I left him behind at the main gate.

The security ordeal clearly wasn't over. There were a few uniformed guards who were randomly checking bags, and I fell prey to that randomness. They went through my baggage with gloved hands, carefully screening the contents with their trained eyes.

You'd think that that would have been the final check. But now the airline insisted on scanning my baggage. Again. I have never been happier to have my bags checked-in and go through the carousel than on that day. I was left with my hand luggage and went through the final security check. Even though the handbags went through X-ray machines, they were manually checked again at the other end before I could pick them up. With a rubber ink stamp on my baggage tag, I stood confidently in front of the staff, expecting to be let through to my boarding gate. But I was now directed towards a 'baggage identification' section that was manned by airline staff and not the CRPF. Once they had manually marked my tag with an X in indelible ink, I was free at last to proceed to the boarding gate.

With fifteen minutes to kill before boarding, and too buzzed from the events of the past few days to sit still, I walked into Gulshan Book Store. The shopkeeper regarded me quizzically at first when I asked for books that would help me understand the history and politics of Kashmir. But then he looked pleased and quickly got me three books. All three had been published by Gulshan Publishers. When I asked if there were books by other publishers, he replied in the negative. This is odd, I thought. Scanning the shelves, I discovered that all the books in the store carried the same imprint. Being an author myself, I couldn't help but ask the shopkeeper about this peculiar phenomenon.

He answered my question with a smile and a shrug, and billed me for my purchase. My flight was announced in the meantime, and I headed for the gate where, to my surprise, another metal detector test awaited me.

As my flight prepared to take off, I bade Kashmir goodbye with a promise to return. I knew that between the sudden death of Lieutenant Ummer Fayaz, the oddities of life in the Valley, and the concept of Kashmiriyat, lay the truth. I had more unanswered questions now than when I had started, but I was determined to get to the bottom of it all.

Chapter 5

Jameela and eight-and-a-half-month-old Ummer returned home to a grand welcome. Fayaz could hardly contain his excitement at having them back in Kulgam; Ummer looked so different now, more animated, engaging and inquisitive about the world around him.

For Jameela, the past months had been busy and exhausting, as it is for all new mothers. She had grown used to taking care of Ummer now, having picked up the skills and gestures of motherhood from the women at her maternal home. She gave Ummer massages and baths, fed him and changed his nappies dozens of times every day quite efficiently. Dreading nappy rashes, she would meticulously dry his nappies by the fire so that he always had fresh, clean ones for the next day. Soon, she also resumed her household chores, including cooking for her in-laws and cleaning the home. It took Fayaz a while to notice that something was amiss, or rather, that his wife had changed.

'You seem here and not so here at the same time, Jameela. I hardly get to see you even though we stay in the same house.'

As if on cue, nine-month-old Ummer started to cry, and Jameela rushed to pacify him. It took a good five minutes to soothe him and another twenty to put him to sleep, rocking him back and forth and gently rubbing his back. Watching her handle Ummer so calmly, Fayaz admired her tenacity to go through the same routine over and over again. Every single day. He knew then that the aura of a woman, especially a mother, is like the warm winter sun. We bask in its comfort, absorbing and soaking in the very essence of it, and don't realize how vital it is to our well-being until it is gone. Fayaz wished he could find a way to pitch in, but he had to spend most of his day in the apple orchard, working hard to ensure the crop was healthy and the fruit in perfect condition to sell in the markets.

Another day, Fayaz came home early for lunch and was thrilled to find Ummer wide awake and crawling around the house. He picked him up, determined to make him say 'papa', repeating the word over and over again, as Ummer observed him with rapt attention. And then he said 'mimi', which was babyspeak for 'ammi' (mother). Jameela burst into peals of laughter while Fayaz faked a frown, shaking his head in mock disgust.

She couldn't help but rub it in, with a smile: 'Children are like the mother's beating heart.'

Ummer was about a year old when he started to walk. Gingerly at first, with the support of furniture, and then with new-found confidence, marching around the house much like the stately soldiers at the Wagah border—lifting one leg high up in the air and stomping it down firmly, only to repeat the action with the other, in a deliberate show of strength. His grandfather was the first to notice the resemblance and remark on it, to the great amusement of the rest of the household.

Jameela could sense Fayaz's longing to be close to his son. To surprise him, she taught Ummer to say 'papa'. One evening, when Fayaz returned home from work, Ummer walked towards him, clung to his leg and called him 'papa'. Finally! His face glowing with happiness and pride, Fayaz perched little Ummer on his shoulders and wouldn't put him down for a long time after.

Ummer's grandmother too had a role in grooming and teaching him new things every day. Fayaz couldn't help but feel proud that his mother and wife were doing a grand job of raising his son. He said that to his wife in as many words. Jameela, however, was quick to disagree.

'There's only so much I can do, Fayaz. There will come a time when he'll need you more than he needs me.'

'Never! Kids always need their mothers more than they do their fathers. Look at me. Almost twenty-eight years old, and I still look to my mother for so much in life.'

Pragmatic as always, Jameela replied, 'Fayaz, you have at least been to school. I am illiterate, and when he starts going to school, you will have to pitch in more.'

'Don't worry. When he's old enough, we'll make sure he gets into the best school. Our son will become a "Sahibji". Right, Sahibji?' he said, addressing Ummer now. 'You are going to become a big, big Sahib, aren't you?'

And the name somehow stuck.

In November 1995, Jameela became pregnant with her second child. When it was time, she left with Ummer for her maternal home, and on 6 June 1996, Ummer welcomed his baby sister to the world. She was named Asmat, the Urdu word for 'pure'. Ummer quickly got used to having her around. All of two years old, he would beg to be allowed to hold Asmat on his lap, and the amused grown-ups would oblige him, though not without supervision. Asmat was the apple of her father's eye, and Ummer doted on her too. It was almost as if he knew that she was soon going to be his new partner in crime.

Pretty soon, they were inseparable, playing together one minute and driving their mother to distraction with their fights the next. When it was time for Ummer to go to school, Fayaz and Jameela worried about Asmat. How would she understand her brother's sudden absences from home, after seeing him around all day? But children are resilient by nature, and Asmat soon adjusted to her brother's new routine, for she knew that Ummer would come back home to her each day.

As a parent, Fayaz was fiercely adamant about three things: Urdu, hygiene and education.

In the biting cold of the Valley, Kashmiris are known to not bathe for days. Fayaz wanted his children to break out of this habit and bring them up like Sahibjis so they would acquire the demeanour of a more educated class. Each morning, Fayaz would heat water for the children, supervising their showers and making sure they brushed their teeth. In the years to come, Ummer and his siblings would often be at an advantage over other kids in the locality because they had a father who thought ahead of his time.

One morning, Ummer was being exceptionally naughty and Jameela had had enough. She asked Fayaz to take the boy with him to the orchard, where he could release his pent-up energy. It happened to be plucking season, and the workers had piled ripe apples in a huge heap in a corner of the orchard. Fayaz, deciding to engage his son in counting the apples, sat Ummer down next to the pile. He taught him to count to ten and instructed him to make small heaps of ten apples each. Ummer was hooked. Back home, he repeated this exercise over and over all day, counting different things he found around the house. First it was the onions and potatoes in the kitchen, then the stones in the garden. He didn't even spare the walnuts in his grandmother's almirah. And that was how Ummer learn the basics of mathematics with his father. He was sharp; it didn't take long for him to learn to count to a hundred. Observing his progress, Fayaz decided to take his son to the next level.

He gave Ummer some apples and asked, 'How many do you have?'

Ummer counted with his small fingers and answered, 'Five'.

'If I take three apples and eat them, how many would you have left?'

Ummer, alarmed, retorted innocently, 'I'm not giving you my apples. They're mine.'

Fayaz struggled to hide his smile as he reframed the question. 'Okay, who do you think you can give three of your apples to?'

After a moment's deep reflection, Ummer lisped, 'Asssma.'

'Why? Because you love her and she's your baby sister?'

'No! Because she has no teeth and can't eat my apples.'

Fayaz laughed his head off, and later recounted this story to Jameela, his parents, and even the extended family.

Asmat was only a year old and Ummer, at three, was acutely aware of his sister's limitations. Tickled as he was at this moment, Fayaz wasn't one to be distracted easily.

'Okay, since Asmat will only play with your apples and give them back to you when you ask, if you gave her three, how many will you have left?'

Ummer set aside three apples and counted what was left. 'Two,' he said.

Fayaz thought his heart would burst with pride. His son had to be the smartest three-year-old in town.

For the next two years, the apple orchard became Ummer's haven of learning. By the age of five, even before entering the portals of a school, Ummer could do basic addition and subtraction, as well as write the letters of the English alphabet in small and capital letters.

Meanwhile, Fayaz and Jameela had begun talking to other parents, and discussing potential schools for their children. Their research was quite thorough, and when it was time for Ummer to begin formal education, they had already scanned all the schools in the area in terms of fees, infrastructure and popularity.

Their heart was set on Hanfia Model School in Kulgam, but Ummer had to clear an entrance test first. Fayaz and Jameela were worried for no reason at all. Equipped with his learnings from the apple orchard, their son sailed through the test. Thus began Ummer's schooling, at the age of five.

One day, a child from Ummer's class lost his geometry box. The teacher called all the students and asked them to swear by the holy Quran that they hadn't stolen it. One by one, each child put their hand on the book placed on the teacher's table and swore. When it was Ummer's turn, he took one look at the book and said, 'Sir, this is a dictionary, not the Quran.' The students started giggling, and the embarrassed teacher grew red in the face. After school, he sought Fayaz out when he came to pick up Ummer, and informed him of his son's cheekiness.

Back at home, Fayaz gave Ummer a dressing-down, but was secretly pleased that his son had spotted what an entire class of children had missed. The power of keen observation is a precious life-skill, something his son possessed in abundance. Calling a spade a spade was an innate trait that Ummer possessed. Even as a little boy, he perceived most things as black or white, and dismissed shades of grey.

The management at Hanfia Model School was liberal, and allowed parents to assist in their children's education as much as they liked. Fayaz would sometimes take on the role of a teacher in Ummer's classroom, much to the delight of all his friends. However, the absence of Urdu in the school curriculum bothered Fayaz. He made several requests to the school authorities, and finally, the principal agreed to introduce it as a proper subject.

Ummer was six when his parents were expecting a third child. This time, because they didn't want to disturb Ummer's schooling, Ummer and Asmat were left behind in Kulgam, and Fayaz's mother stepped up to help with the children while Jameela was away at her maternal home. On 15 February 2001, baby Usma arrived. True to her name, she was their beam of sunshine, and her small face radiated warmth. Ummer, now older and more aware, was fascinated with this little being.

Two years after Ummer, Asmat joined Hanfia Model School which was just a five-minute walk from their home. The siblings got to spend more time together and grew even closer. To make sure that Ummer was getting the most out of his education, Fayaz engaged an after-school tuition teacher, trading some apples for an hour of the teacher's time. Ummer would come home from school, have lunch and then head out to the teacher's house. On the third day, he didn't return home at the expected time. Terrified, the family went looking for him in all directions. Jameela was pregnant with her third child. The situation in the Valley wasn't very different in those days from what it is now, and there were cases of children being kidnapped to be trained as terrorists. None of the abducted children ever came back home. The day young Ummer disappeared, everyone feared the worst, although no one in the family would say it out loud.

They searched high and low for hours until it was dark, but found no trace of the boy. Jameela, five months pregnant, was worried out of her wits. She pleaded with her husband to register a complaint with the police, but Fayaz was reluctant. The police coming home, even in the given circumstance, could spell trouble in the place they lived.

At around 7 p.m. that evening, a sleepy-eyed Ummer sauntered out of their storeroom on the third floor, wondering what all the chaos was about. He had hidden himself there earlier in the afternoon and had eventually fallen asleep out of boredom. Needless to say, he was thoroughly scolded by the grown-ups in the house. They were immensely relieved, but justifiably angry at the mischievousness that had made subsequent hours hellish.

Realizing that everyone was upset because of him, a guilt-stricken Ummer explained, 'Papa, that teacher doesn't know how to teach. I feel like I know more than him. I don't want to go there any more.'

Fayaz wondered what could be so wrong with the teacher that little Ummer was so adamant about not resuming his tuition. He, however, trusted his son's judgement.

'If you are not happy with the teacher, you don't have to go there again,' he calmly told his son.

At age eight, Ummer was quite a handful; he and Asmat were always up to no good. Fayaz's uncle, Hassan Parrey, lived next door and had a haystack in his backyard. It was meant to be fodder for the cows he owned. One day, Ummer waited until dusk and then instructed Asmat to bring a matchbox from the kitchen.

'Why, Sahibji?' Asmat asked innocently, using the family nickname for Ummer.

'Don't argue, just do it.'

Used to taking orders from her older brother, Asmat complied and handed the matchbox over to Ummer. Once at the scene of the crime, Ummer acted quickly. He couldn't get the first match to light and the stick broke. But he struck gold with the next one, and flicked the burning match into the heap of hay. It caught fire instantly, and in no time, most of the backyard was up in flames. Hassan and his family came rushing out to see the two little arsonists jumping up and down in glee. As soon as the duo spotted their uncle, however, Ummer grabbed his accomplice's hand and ran back to his own house.

Meanwhile Fayaz, spotting the fire, had rushed out to help. On learning that Ummer and Asmat had started it, he was livid. Summoning the two miscreants, he told them in no uncertain terms that he was extremely disappointed in them. Asmat was young, he conceded, but Ummer should have known better. Ummer successfully feigned a guilty look while Asmat, who had no clue what was happening, stood stoically next to her brother, chin raised in defiance, forever his ardent supporter.

Sensing that they had crossed a limit this time, they were quick to obey when Fayaz ordered them to apologize to Uncle Hassan. Jameela, now several months into her fourth pregnancy, felt a little guilty for having neglected her older children. Uncle Hassan, however, was more concerned than angry.

'Damage can be mended. We'll clean it up tomorrow. But what if something happened to you two? Do you two little fools not know that fire also burns people?'

'Sorry, Chacha,' Asmat and Ummer chimed in unison.

But their shenanigans did not stop there, and poor Uncle Hassan somehow always ended up bearing the brunt of their mischief. For her fourth delivery, Jameela left Ummer and Asmat behind but took Usma with her to Batpora, as she was too young to be entrusted to the care of Fayaz's ageing parents. By then, Jameela had mastered the art of giving birth and didn't need much assistance. On 3 March 2003, the Parrey family was blessed with a little blue-eyed girl whom they named Nargis. According to Jameela, she was the prettiest of all her children.

Soon after Nargis's birth, Jameela observed something peculiar about her. The baby did not seem able to discharge urine and her stomach was swollen. Jameela and Fayaz immediately took Nargis to the nearest hospital where the doctor informed them that their daughter was suffering from a nervous disorder. The nerves responsible for urination were not able to coordinate between the bladder, the spinal cord and the brain, leading to urine retention in the bladder.

Nargis was put on medication straight away, and thenceforth, urine had to be removed artificially from her bladder. It caused Fayaz and Jameela untold pain to see their daughter attached constantly to a catheter and urine drainage bag. Jameela's attention was completely focused on Nargis now, and she wasn't left with much time or energy for her older children. The baby had to be taken to the doctor often, for medication and urine bag changes. The family gradually got used to Nargis's condition. Her siblings adored her and willingly helped their mother take good care of her. The doctors, however, knew that the child would not survive for long.

During this time, Ummer had grown very close to both his grandmothers. Once, when he was barely ten, he missed his maternal grandmother so terribly that he decided he couldn't wait for vacations and would go visit her all by himself. His plan was to walk to Batpora, taking a shortcut through the forest to get there faster. The woods were thick and forbidding; even adults rarely ventured into them alone. But the young, naïve Ummer set out with his grandfather's walking stick, and walked and walked. On the way, he came across a jackal which advanced menacingly towards him. He gathered the courage to throw a stone at the animal, and it fled. Luckily, it didn't come back to bother him. Eventually, Ummer reached his grandmother's home.

Maqbool was shocked to see his nephew at the front door with no parents in tow. When he learnt that Ummer had walked through the jungle and hadn't informed his parents of his plan, Maqbool immediately called to let them know where Ummer was. Speechless with disbelief at first, Fayaz and Jameela were predictably agitated by their son's exploit, but then Maqbool pointed out that the boy must have really missed his grandma and asked them to let him stay for a few days. He promised to bring Ummer back to Kulgam himself. On returning home, Ummer excitedly narrated his adventure to the family. His grandfather said, 'Sahibji, you are no doubt a brave boy, but there is a thin line between bravery and foolishness. If you had gotten lost or if the jackal had attacked you, people would certainly have called you foolish. Now, can I please have my walking stick back?'

One day, Fayaz noticed that his father was having trouble walking and thought it might help to get him a new walking stick. He asked Ummer to go to the market and get one. 'Take Asmat with you,' he ordered. Asmat, always eager to spend time with Ummer, tagged along because an outing with her older brother never failed to offer an adventure. Brand new walking stick in hand, they were on their way home when Ummer had a brainwave. He instructed Asmat to hold one end of the stick from across the road, while he held the other.

'This is an army barricade now,' he declared. 'If anyone wants to pass, they have to show us their IDs first.'

That very moment, they saw a man on a scooter approaching them. Instead of letting go of the stick, Ummer commanded Asmat to lift it. But his assessment of their own height was way off the mark. The rider, in an attempt to avoid the 'barricade', veered and crashed on the side of the road. Of course, Ummer and Asmat bolted from the scene, dropping the walking stick on the road.

But they had run out of luck. The man on the scooter was none other than Uncle Hassan, and sure enough, he came limping to Fayaz, walking stick in tow.

'This *naar chor* will have me killed one day,' he complained, grimacing in pain from the bruises on his body. *Naar* means 'fire' in Kashmiri, and *chor* means 'thief'. From that day on, Uncle Hassan called Ummer 'Naar Chor'.

Fayaz however, concerned about his children's lack of discipline, decided to confront Jameela about a matter that had long been weighing on his mind.

'Don't you think you're too occupied with Nargis and not paying enough attention to our other children? They need you too.'

A teary-eyed Jameela looked at baby Nargis and said, 'She's too little to endure all this. My daughter is suffering, Fayaz. She is dying!'

Jameela wept profusely, and Fayaz took her in his arms, rubbing his cheek against her tear-stained face. He then cupped her face with his hands, kissed her on the forehead, and did not utter another word. The next day, they took Nargis to the doctor, who advised them to prepare for the worst.

'Her condition is deteriorating. I don't think she has much time left.'

Jameela and Fayaz already knew the inevitable, but no matter how certain death is, when it comes, it takes a toll on the spirit that no one is prepared for. In 2005, Fayaz's family lost their beloved daughter Nargis.

Ummer, Asmat and Usma were now the centre of Jameela and Fayaz's universe, lending meaning to their lives and giving them the strength and purpose to become the best parents they could possibly be.

Chapter 6

Lieutenant Ummer Fayaz was a commissioned officer of 2 Raj Rif, a prestigious unit of the celebrated Rajputana Rifles regiment. Before I tell you more about the unit, do you remember those who were killed in action in the Kargil War? Just to refresh your memory, 527 were reported dead and 1363 wounded. This was the official figure for casualties on the Indian side. When I heard that Ummer's unit was 2 Raj Rif, I fondly remembered a brave captain from the same unit, Captain Vijayant Thapar. The emotional 'last letter' he wrote to his family from the Kargil front had moved the entire nation. I distinctly recalled a line, 'As far as the unit is concerned, the new chaps should be told about this sacrifice.'*

Not everyone who joins the army is initially motivated by patriotism or a sense of national pride, but in the course of their military training and induction into a unit, they are exposed to so many examples of the supreme sacrifice that the words of those killed in action soon begin to flow in their very veins. We mourn the slaying of our soldiers, but there really is no better way to meet death than by laying

---

* https://www.captainvijyantthapar.com/lastletter.html

your life down for the motherland. People who offer, suffer or even witness such sacrifices know this better than I do and will agree with me.

On 31 August 2017, I got permission to visit Lieutenant Ummer's unit, 2 Raj Rif, which was then posted in Keri, along the LoC. I was allowed to interview a few officers and jawans who served with him.

I took a flight to Jammu and then hired a taxi to take me to Akhnoor, which is about a forty-minute drive from the city. From Akhnoor, Keri is another three hours away. I wasn't allowed a night stay at the LoC as it was against security procedures of the army.

While I was on my way, I received a message on my mobile from Colonel Rohit Bharwe, the commanding officer of 2 Raj Rif:

'Hope you've landed safely ma'am! The only means of conversation with me would be WhatsApp.'

'The pilot did make sure of that, Col Rohit.' I texted in reply, with a smiley.

'It's been raining cats and dogs here, ma'am and one of the nullahs is overflowing. Hope it gets cleared by tomorrow, else it'll be difficult for you to cross it and come.'

'I can swim.'

I was dead serious, but Colonel Rohit replied with a laughing emoji.

The Military Intelligence (MI) clearance had taken its own sweet time and I was now impatient to get all the information I could before I started writing. I'm sure my high motivation levels rubbed off a little on the Colonel.

He texted, 'Don't worry ma'am. You're dealing with the Indian Army. We'll make sure that you reach us here tomorrow.'

I could sense the reassuring smile on his face and messaged him my sincerest thanks. I stayed in Akhnoor that night and left the next morning for Keri after catching up on some much-needed rest. Before setting out, I received another message from Colonel Rohit that said, 'We shall see you in a few hours ma'am.'

He explained the route ahead to me, and my worst fears were confirmed when I learnt that we would traverse some extremely steep hilly terrain. The severity of motion sickness increases triplefold on mountain roads. But this time I was carrying some medicine to fight the nausea. I popped a pill, spread a shawl on the back seat of the car and lay down. But sleep wouldn't come easily, so I started a conversation with the driver.

'Bhaiyaji, what's your name?'

'Satnam,' he answered with a smile.

'Where are you from?'

'From Jammu, madam.'

Meanwhile I had found a newspaper lying next to the car's gearbox.

An article on the front page read:

'The National Investigation Agency (NIA) on Sunday raided a Jammu-based advocate's residence and questioned him as part of the agency's crackdown on separatists on the basis of an FIR accusing them of fomenting unrest in Kashmir with funds received from Pakistan-based terror outfits. Devinder Singh Behl is believed to be a close aide of Hurriyat leader Syed Ali Shah Geelani.'

'Devinder Singh Behl's house raided!' I said loudly.

'Yes madam, he was from Jammu. It's a very good step by the central government. Modiji has done it. These bastards were ruining our state. They tried their best to create unrest in Jammu too, but failed miserably,' he said proudly.

'Why do you think they failed?' I wanted to know more, while wondering about the trust the common man seemed to place in Modiji.

'It's because we are Dogra Hindus. Peace and harmony are sacred to us. Our belief system is very different from their belief system. Most of the pandits, when they got kicked out of the Valley, had no option but to settle in Jammu. Why will pandits align with them? The people of the plains usually don't trust the people from the hills, that too when they belong to a different religion.' He shrugged.

'But this guy is a Sikh!' I said, pointing at the picture of Devinder Singh Behl.

'Money has no religion, madam.'

I couldn't have agreed more. My attempt to finish reading the article triggered the inevitable nausea.

I asked Satnam to stop the vehicle, leapt out and threw up. The medicine clearly wasn't working. Satnam handed over a bottle of water from a distance, repulsed by the vomit. We stood on the side of the road, taking a break for a few minutes. Just as I was checking for some signal on the mobile to call my mother, she called me.

'Where are you? Do you even bother to inform me if you're safe? What sort of reckless behaviour is this?' She went on in this vein for a while.

'But Maa . . .' I tried to interject.

'What Maa? I'm trying your number for the past one hour. That silly woman kept telling me that you're out of range.'

'Maa, the network coverage is awful here.'

'So you should have called me when you had network coverage.'

'I'm sorry, Maa!' If you ask me, that is another great way of ending an argument—just tie it up neatly with a meek apology!

'Have you reached?' She mellowed immediately.

'I was just taking a break. Another hour maybe.'

'Don't stand at the LoC. Do you hear me?'

I didn't know whether to laugh or cry, so I cried out laughing. My mom is sweet. Then followed a warm conversation in Punjabi, and soon Satnam and I resumed our journey. My mother's voice worked better than the pill, and I went off to sleep in the car. We were a few metres short of that nullah, when I woke up and saw Colonel Rohit's message.

'Ma'am, the nullah is overflowing. A patch of the road is covered with three feet of water.'

My heart sank but I resolved to cross that nullah, even if it meant I had to swim across.

'Not to worry Col Rohit, I'm carrying a swimming costume with me.' He sent more laughing emojis with another message that read, 'Ma'am, as you reach the nullah, you'll see a post there. In case your car can't cross, we will send a Tatra. You hop into it and come. After you're finished here, the same vehicle will drop you back to the post. Your driver can wait there. He will be taken care of.'

After that message, we couldn't communicate. I had no network on my phone.

Now in case you're wondering what a Tatra is, it's a truck, over ten feet in height. Manufactured by a Czech Republic company called Tatra, these vehicles are used by about thirty-eight armies across the world. The Indian Army uses the 8x8 version. It has a left-hand drive, and can operate in extreme weather conditions ranging from −40°C to +55°C. In short, it is a rather cool truck, and sitting in one is probably the closest you will get to feeling like a superhero, or god! Only a few kilometres from the nullah, we passed a wall that had something written on it: 'It is glory to die doing one's duty.' I asked the driver to stop in order to take a closer look, but he refused.

'Madam, this is the LoC. During the Kargil War, this wall was built to block enemy bullets from Pakistan.'

Suddenly, my mother's words rang in my ear. I regretted laughing at her; she had been right.

When I reached the appointed place, Colonel Rohit was there to receive me.

'Hope your journey was comfortable, ma'am!' he said, shaking hands with me.

'It was all right, thank you for asking!' I was trying to check if there was some signal reception on my phone.

'Ma'am, I suggest you keep your phone in your bag. There's no network here.'

'How do you survive?' I was incredulous.

'We have our ways, ma'am,' said the colonel, with a cryptic smile. 'You can freshen up if you like, before we start the interviews. I've arranged for you to speak to one JCO, three jawans and two officers. After you finish with them, you can come to my office.'

I was quite satisfied with the number of interviewees I had been allocated. The more the people, the more the stories, I told myself as I freshened up in a matter of minutes. Soon, I was in a room where I would interact, one after another, with several people who had been associated with and interacted with Ummer Fayaz at close quarters. It is an extraordinary feeling, to meet a person who knows the person you want to know everything about. It turned out, however, that these soldiers didn't have much to tell me. Ummer had only spent two months with them, that too on a highly sensitive posting just a few metres shy of the LoC. Yet, whatever they did share added vital, if small, pieces to the jigsaw picture I was beginning to form of the life and death of my subject.

After finishing the interviews, I went, as instructed, to the CO's office. Colonel Rohit was on a call, but hung up as soon as I entered his office. Obviously, he did not wish to discuss anything of a confidential or sensitive nature in my presence. It was a tactic I was quite used to by then.

'So ma'am, any luck?' Colonel Rohit offered me a chair.

'Not much.' I sat, pensively joining my palms on the table in front of me.

'Actually, he was with us for only two months. It's too short a time for anyone to gauge the character of a person.' I nodded in affirmation, and the CO continued, 'But whatever we do know of him, is all incredible. His death is a great loss for both the regiment and the army. He was the baby of the unit, you see. Just twenty-two.'

'I understand.'

I recalled that the display picture on Colonel Rohit's WhatsApp account was a photograph of Ummer. It had surprised me a little, but in the light of these words, the CO's gesture seemed both touching and natural.

The colonel's landline rang again; he picked it up only to reply in a grave tone, 'Okay, I'll get back in some time.'

'Everything all right?' I asked, noticing his expression had changed.

'We lost a boy at the LoC a few days back. The call was regarding that.'

'How did he die?'

'He was getting out of the bunker for a duty shift. Some terrorists, who we later learnt had been hiding out in the nearby jungle for a few days, shot him.' Colonel Rohit's tone was neutral, but I could sense that he wasn't very happy about narrating this incident.

'So these kind of incidents keep happening here?' I probed.

'Off and on, when there is a ceasefire violation from their end.' He meant Pakistan, obviously, and I recollected with a start that they were right there, at the LoC.

'We never do it?' 'We' meant India, of course.

'We never violate ceasefire agreements, but if they fire, we have to retaliate.' He smiled and shrugged. 'That's why we denied permission for you to stay the night here. Firstly, it would have been against the rules, and secondly, you would have been the only person in the area without a sanctioned weapon. But unfortunately for us, it's the pen that changes things and not the gun. Our power is severely limited.'

Perceiving the disappointment and frustration on Colonel Rohit's face, I felt a pang of empathy.

'What's sadder is that you use your power only in defence, after you've lost a few. Being defensive, the best you can hope for is a tie. Never a win. History is proof,' he said.

'But the truth is that no one has ever won anything by being offensive either. History yet again is proof.'

He was right, but then it was something of a never-ending debate, like the chicken-and-egg question.

'Do you think that we will ever be able to attain peace?'

I felt completely stupid the moment I asked this question, but was convinced by the CO's reply.

'Peace is not in the hands of the defender, ma'am. It is always in the hands of the aggressor. India's defence budget is only 1.17 per cent of its GDP whereas Pakistan spends 2.81 per cent of its total GDP on the defence sector. Why do they need this kind of money for defence when we have never initiated a war with Pakistan till date?'

I looked blankly at Colonel Rohit, waiting for an answer.

'You should see the way the armed forces live in Pakistan! They maintain obscenely high standards of living and are easily one of the richest professional communities in the country. How are these lifestyles sustained? By paying huge salaries. And the justification for these excesses is provided by first creating tensions and then crying victim. The Pakistan Army has been able to convince their people that they are all that stand between the citizens and an Indian conquest, whereas the truth is that all we do is retaliate and die.'

Everything seemed to make better sense now. When a lie is repeated often enough, it takes on the appearance of truth. This happens in India as well, but democracy, to an extent, keeps a check on these mechanisms of deception.

After some more conversation on Pakistan, India and Ummer, the CO and I went to the officers' mess for lunch. Just as I was about to sit down, Colonel Rohit called me into a small, makeshift library adjoining the mess.

'Before Ummer went on leave,' the colonel said, 'I'd asked him to classify these books genre-wise.'

I approached the glass cabinet that contained the books. They were impeccably sorted and arranged according to genres.

'I met him over dinner one night and asked him to complete this task. He was supposed to go on leave the very next day—that leave from which he never returned. Nevertheless, he sat up the whole night to finish the task and left with the early morning convoy.'

There was a look of pride on the CO's face. 'You were harsh on the poor boy.'

I suddenly pictured Ummer staying awake the entire night to perform this tedious task.

'I never meant that he should do the task that same night. But he was a dutiful officer, and I'm very happy that he obeyed my command, else I wouldn't have been able to show you this today.'

As I took a few pictures of the book cabinet, I heard Colonel Rohit say, almost to himself, 'We will make sure we maintain this classification.'

Just then, the mess havaldar came to tell us that lunch was ready. As we sat down to our meals, a potentially offensive question popped into my head, 'Don't take offence, Colonel. I know that the Indian Army is a secular organization, but I can't help asking this question. Did you ever suspect Lieutenant Ummer's loyalties, for being a Kashmiri who hailed from such a disturbed area?'

The CO looked at me as if it was the first time such a question had been put to him, and as if he had never ever paid attention to that fact.

'I wish I had paid more attention to the fact that he came from a disturbed area. His being a Kashmiri wasn't an issue at all. The selection process at the SSB (Service Selection Board) level is pretty foolproof. There are many officers and jawans from Kashmir, maybe fewer from that particular area, but there are. We never expected anything like this to happen.' He shrugged and continued, 'Ma'am, my unit is Raj Rif. Fifty per cent are Jats from Haryana, and the rest are mostly Rajputs from Rajasthan. If we go by Indian history, these are two of the country's most martial communities. But we've had COs and other officers from all states and religions. That's the spirit of the Indian Army. I couldn't have possibly doubted or questioned that spirit by baselessly suspecting an officer. The moles usually get shunted during the selection process or the training process. Once a soldier becomes an officer, it means he has stood the test of loyalty.'

I completely understood his view of the matter.

'Was there a possibility that you could have stopped him from going on leave?'

While researching a story like this, you develop a tendency to evaluate possibilities that might have saved the man who died. Every time I spoke to someone who knew him in life, I felt this urge to pull Ummer out of the jaws of death. Maybe that's what happens when you get emotionally involved in a story.

'We only stop men or officers going on leave when there is a shortage of manpower or an eventuality of conflict. When Ummer applied for leave, there was none. I had no reason to stop him, and he never told me that his area was so disturbed. We didn't see any potential threat to his life. And ma'am, how long can someone avoid going to his own home?'

I nodded mutely in affirmation. Under normal circumstances, what place could be safer than one's hometown, or a house filled with friends and family on a joyous occasion? There had been no reason for Ummer to not go home for his cousin's wedding, and no reason for Colonel Rohit to stop him. We resumed our meal. I ate very little for fear of motion sickness overwhelming me on the journey back. After lunch, we returned to Colonel Rohit's office and spoke a little more about his unit and Ummer. Finally, I took his leave, and he called for a vehicle to drop me back to my taxi.

This time it was a Gypsy, as Colonel Rohit had already been informed that the water in the nullah had receded. I was impressed with this instance of efficient communication at various levels in the army. But the child in me had wanted to ride the Tatra again, and I was deeply disappointed. I was dropped off at the entry post where my taxi was parked.

On my way back, I was more at ease in my mind. I quietly watched the changing landscape through the car's windows, observing the tiny huts and small houses, few and far between, the tea stalls, groceries and mechanic shops at long intervals. The sight of a few locals walking alongside their laden ponies triggered my curiosity.

'Who are they, Satnam bhaiya?' I asked, pointing.

'Oh, they're porters, madam. They carry rations, oil and other supplies for the soldiers at the post.'

'Can't vehicles be used to transport the supplies?'

'For some posts, yes, but to reach others that are inaccessible by road, one needs these porters. That's one of the major livelihoods of the villagers in these parts, apart from small-time farming.'

'What if one of the porters turns out to be a terrorist?' Questions of trust and mistrust loomed large in my mind that day.

'They have valid ID cards, madam. They're checked for security. And the army punishes those who are caught deceiving them.'

'But what's the point, after the damage is done? Precaution is better than cure,' I reasoned.

'Madam, there is no other way. The soldiers can't survive without the rations. This risk is worth taking, for the basic necessities of life. How will a soldier fight on an empty stomach?'

'How do you know so much about the army, Satnam?'

'Two of my three sons are in the army, madam. One of them is at the border and the other is in Rajasthan,' he said proudly.

'What about your third son?'

'We didn't let him join the army; we want at least one of them to stay with us. We are growing old now, madam.'

Satnam must have been in his late sixties, I realized, but seemed relatively strong and active for his age.

'I'm getting him married tomorrow,' Satnam mentioned.

'That's wonderful.'

I was craving tea, and asked him to stop at a local teashop. We passed one just then but he refused to stop, stating that the shop belonged to a Muslim. I wondered whether the teashop where we finally stopped used water from the Ganges to make tea, but wisely kept this thought to myself. When we reached my place in Srinagar that night, Satnam bid me goodbye while handing my luggage over.

'Madam, tomorrow I'll send my associate to drop you off at the airport. I won't be able to come.'

Suddenly reminded that it was Satnam's son's wedding the next day, I said, 'Oh! Congratulations and good wishes to you and your family.'

The day's activities had exhausted me, and I had an early flight the next morning. Skipping dinner, I went straight to bed. When I was all packed up for the airport the following day, there was a punctual knock on the door.

'Madam, my name is Nazir. Satnam has sent me to take you to the airport. Are you ready?'

All the way, I wondered why Satnam, who supposedly hated Muslims so much, had a Muslim man working for him. I resolved to call the next day, on the pretext of congratulating him on his son's wedding, and ask.

'Satnam bhaiya, you didn't let me have a cup of tea at a Muslim shop, but you have a Muslim employee. How come?'

'Are you talking about Nazir?'

'Yes.'

'Madam, he is not exactly a Muslim. His forefathers were Hindus, but his grandparents converted to Islam. Nazir himself doesn't practise the faith. That's what Indian Muslims are about, all converted. His name is Nazir Pandit. Now you tell me, who has a name like that?'

'Satnam bhaiya, if I were a Muslim, would you have taken me in your car?'

'Madamji, when it comes to a choice between religion and livelihood, bread and butter always wins,' he laughed.

I thanked him and hung up, surprised at the sharp clarity of the practical distinctions he had made. 'But there's a thought,' I reflected. 'Commerce can exist between anyone, unlike deeper affiliations. If we can't attain peace through religion, perhaps we should focus on commerce. Let economics erase a divisive history.'

Chapter 7

Before Ummer's parents had realized it, he was eleven years old and had completed Class V. It was now time for them to look for a school that had more to offer their son than the one he was currently attending. No effort or expense was spared in preparing Ummer for the entrance examination to the Jawahar Navodaya Vidyalaya (JNV).[*] For parents in the Valley's villages, the upward mobility they aspire to for their children is all about transitioning to an urban lifestyle. And schools like JNV are ideal stepping-stones for families like Ummer's. Fayaz brought home books with reams of questions and problems for his son to solve. Just about everything was done to help Ummer face D-Day.

Like most Kashmiri kids his age, Ummer was crazy about cricket. A small cricket factory in Halmulla, renowned for its fine bats made from Kashmir willow, fed the cricket craze in their part of the Valley. Although the

---

[*] JNVs are fully residential and co-educational schools affiliated to the Central Board of Secondary Education (CBSE), New Delhi, with classes from Class VI to XII. JNVs are specifically tasked with finding talented children in rural areas of India and providing them with an education equivalent to the best residential school system, without regard to their families' socio-economic condition.

national sport in India as well as Pakistan happens to be hockey, it can't be denied that cricket remains by far the more popular sport in both countries. When the Indian and Pakistani teams play against each other, it is hard to ignore the troubled currents of history that underlie their rivalry on the pitch. And even if the players do manage occasionally to transcend this, the frenzied fans on either side would invariably remind them of it.

It was 2 April 2005, the day of Ummer's entrance exam. It was also the first ODI match of the series between India and Pakistan. Fayaz gently tried to shake Ummer out of a deep slumber.

'Wake up, Sahibji. Your exam is today. This could be the beginning of the rest of your life.'

A good education has the potential to change lives. And for a middle-class Kashmiri man with peace in his heart, education was a weapon of self-defence. Fayaz wanted his son to be equipped with a sharp one.

'Five more minutes, Papa,' Ummer begged. He had succeeded in turning his Ammi into a sort of snooze alarm, as Jameela could still hardly bear to wake her sleeping child. But Fayaz would have none of it.

'Not a minute more. You've already slept an extra half-hour. Wake up or I'll throw a bucket of cold water on your head.'

Ummer knew this was no empty threat. With some effort, he forced himself out of bed and overdid the 'sleepy walk' to the bathroom in a bid to gain his father's sympathy. Halfway there, he suddenly straightened up. All sleep seemed to have vanished into thin air. Fayaz watched with complete disdain; he knew what had jogged his son's memory. Ummer ran to the living room and switched on the TV. A sports channel was airing the India–Pakistan match series. Pakistan was touring India, and the match was being played at Kochi. India won the toss and elected to bat first. Ummer's eyes were now glued to the screen.

Fayaz was a wise father, and knew how to pick his battles. Such a crucial match was not something to dismiss, exam or no exam.

'Son, will you please just get ready! We have to reach Anantnag for your exam, and we'll be late if you continue to watch this.'

Repeating this admonition in a louder and firmer voice did the trick. Ummer, craning his neck towards the screen for as long as he could, tore himself away from the room and had a shower in record time. Then he was back in front of the TV, a towel wrapped around his waist.

Sehwag and Tendulkar were the opening pair of batsmen. Ummer was transfixed, and Fayaz didn't have the heart to blame him. He wished deep inside that the exam wasn't today of all days, and that he could just watch the match with his son. But he knew that this temptation to indulge his son wouldn't help Ummer in the long run.

'Ummer, how many times do I have to repeat the same thing?'

Just then, Sachin hit a ball in the air. The bowler, Naved-ul-Hasan, was ecstatic when Yousuf Youhana caught the ball, effectively sending Sachin back to the pavilion.

'See Papa, Sachin is out because of you. You shouldn't interrupt when Sachin is batting,' cried Ummer.

'I am not interrupting Sachin. I am interrupting you. Now put on your clothes and get your things. We need to leave. *Now*.'

Fayaz switched off the TV to make his point. He watched as his son half-heartedly got up, and tossed him his clothes. Still in game mode, Ummer caught them with one hand, showing off his fielding skills. After a quick breakfast, Fayaz let his son update himself on the score by turning on the TV one last time. Captain Ganguly was out for a duck, and Dravid had replaced him. The latter was playing his characteristic game, slow but steady. Having memorized the score and with a heart pounding for the outcome of the match, Ummer finally left for Anantnag with his father on a journey that was meant to change his life. Change was certain; whether for better or worse, only time would tell.

The entrance exam was being held at the school. On reaching their destination, Ummer checked the roll number on his admit card, and tallying it with the seat allotments, gauged that his seat was in Class XII on the first floor. Meanwhile Fayaz, the ever-cautious father, reconfirmed these details with the peon.

Making sure Ummer was seated in time for his exam, Fayaz made his way to the waiting room. Luckily for him, the room had a TV and an assortment of other fathers were glued to the screen. Fayaz was grateful for the distraction; the match would take his mind off Ummer and the exam.

It was a motley crew of fans: some were rooting for the Pakistani team while others cheered for their favourite Indian player, and a few were watching just for the fun of the game. Clearly there was a lack of consensus, which could probably be traced to the disjuncture between the national and religious identities of the viewers. This division of loyalties between the Indian and Pakistani cricket teams among a small group of men watching a match on TV in a school waiting room in Anantnag signalled a deeper divide, in fact, a split sense of identity, or a sort of identity crisis, in the Kashmiri psyche, which has its roots in a long history of conflict.

A loud thud at the stumps marked the end of Dravid's innings. He was run out by Mohammed Sami. Predictably, this provoked mixed reactions in the waiting room that day. Some were evidently happy while others looked disappointed, and a few were clearly unsure of how they felt. Too nervous to enjoy the game, Fayaz got up and walked to the classroom where Ummer was writing his exam. At some point, Ummer looked up to see his father watching him. Fayaz was rewarded by a quick smile from his son before he plunged back into his paper.

Ummer finished the first half of the exam with a half hour to spare, and quite predictably, ran to the waiting room just in time to watch Dhoni play. Dhoni was not yet an established player and had been in the team for just a few months. He was out quickly. Ummer's heart was now set on another favourite, Shahid Afridi of Pakistan. There was an hour's break before the second part of the exam, during which he did not once take his eyes off the screen. He left in time for the rest of the exam, finished early, and raced back to the waiting room.

'What is wrong with you? How did you come out so soon? Have you written everything?' Fayaz shot a volley of questions at Ummer.

'Yes, papa! What's the score now?' Ummer tried frantically to make his way through the crowd in front of the TV to look at the score.

'Couldn't you have gone through your answers once again instead of running out like that?' Fayaz admonished.

'Papa, I'll make it. I've done very well. I always do, when I watch a cricket match.'

Was his son being confident or bumptious? Fayaz would find out soon enough.

India won the match, and Sehwag's performance elevated him to the rank of Ummer's new favourite player of the season. The boy's choices in these matters were always performance-driven, unlike some of the adults in the TV room that day whose loyalties were decided by politics. When one of his favourites was playing, it didn't matter which team he belonged to. This fair and neutral attitude was due in large measure to his thoughtful upbringing. Fayaz and Jameela took care to focus on Ummer's education and instil values of sportsmanship while weeding out any elements of malice bred by exposure to the divisive politics of the Valley.

A month later, the results of the entrance exam were declared. Ummer had made it in his first attempt! Weeks later, he was sent to Anantnag with a trunk full of clothes, toiletries, books, stationery and bedding. Fayaz and Jameela were happy and proud but it was one of toughest things they had had to do since Ummer was born—dropping him off at a boarding school, fully aware of the fact that they would no longer be able to see him every day. However, they knew that the move was in their son's best interests.

Besides, the thought that Asmat and Usma, who continued to study in the Kulgam school, would remain at home with them a while longer offered some consolation.

JNV was drastically different from what Ummer was used to at his former school. The day started a lot earlier, to begin with, and was filled with activity, some of which involved independent work or study. They had PT sessions in the morning, followed by prayers, parade and regular classes. Then there was a study period, where he was expected to work on his own. It all took some getting used to, but Ummer was eager to learn, do well and make his family proud. He soon became a happy, well-adjusted and ambitious student. Boarding school is not for everyone, but sometimes in life, the right path chooses you, and this certainly seemed to be happening in Ummer's case.

The kids at JNV came from diverse backgrounds. Some belonged to affluent families while others had working-class parents. Ummer always had a soft corner for the boys who looked a little blue or out of place. He had the knack for befriending these lost souls and cheering them up without making a big deal of it. Although he had many friends, his best buddies were Javed Shaikh and Zainub Khan. Growing up together at JNV, they shared adolescent pangs as well as thrills, and made many memories of which the sweet outweighed the bitter.

What stood out for his teachers during those years was Ummer's unswerving gumption to question and reason. This trait was evident in his early childhood—for instance, when he decided that he didn't want to be tutored by an incapable teacher, or when he pointed out to his teacher at school that the book he made them swear on was a dictionary and not the Holy Quran. Even as a small child, Ummer didn't appreciate lies. But a passion for truth sometimes comes at a price. Ummer had no inkling of what this virtue was going to cost him.

Ummer's friend Javed, too, came from a poor family. But Javed's parents, like Fayaz and Jameela, dreamt of a better life for their son and placed their hope in a good education as a means of making it possible. As Ummer, Javed and Zainub grew older, their childhood friendship was forged into a deep bond of brotherhood. And due to their growing exposure to the politics of the state, it was natural and inevitable that their young minds would form opinions of their own on the Indian military presence in Kashmir.

Three years into JNV, on the first day of Ummer's first term in Class VIII, the school opened to disturbing news. A senior, Afsal Qureshi of Class XI, was reported missing. By all accounts, he had disappeared on his way to school. The first thing the staff did was to report the matter to the police, only to be informed that the police themselves had detained him for misbehaving with an army jawan. Intense negotiations with the police followed, and after a round of apologies, he was allowed to return to school in the evening. All the students were itching to know what had happened. But they knew better than to violate the decorum of study time and dinner. Soon after the teachers left, they crowded around Afsal. His face had turned a deep crimson.

'Are you okay?' Afsal's classmate, Rahim Iqbal, ventured. That was enough to set his friend off on an agitated rant.

'What do they think of themselves? They don't even know that Anantnag is also called Islamabad. And they think they can rule us, the first citizens of this state.'

Rahim's political affiliations became evident, as he fuelled Afsal's anger: 'Of course, they know it is called Islamabad. They just don't want us to use the name because it also happens to be the capital of Pakistan. Just another tactic to suppress us. But we won't let that happen.'

The room was filled with kids that had grown up with slogans of azadi. Every time there was a crisis in the law-and-order situation, the call for azadi rang loud and clear on the streets. A stirring slogan indeed, but its meaning was as yet unclear in the context of the future of the Kashmiri people. Whether those who promoted these slogans had anything concrete to offer Kashmir once it attained azadi remained to be seen.

That night a heated discussion went on among the boys for hours. Predictably, there was no attempt to consider the facts from both sides, and the army emerged as the villain of the piece.

'Lights out,' shouted the warden eventually, and the students scrambled to their beds, only to fall into a fitful sleep, agitated by the seeming injustice of it all.

When all the students had gone to bed, Afsal opened his eyes to find Ummer sitting at the foot of his.

'You picked that fight deliberately, right? You knew that the word "Islamabad" annoys and provokes those men in uniform because there are so many militants in the area. They might even have suspected you of being a young militant on a suicide mission of sorts. What did you gain from doing it, except a reddened face?' Ummer then looked at Afsal's face more closely and took a dig at him, 'Hope they reddened only your face and nothing else.'

Afsal knew Ummer was speaking the truth, so he chose not to answer, although the expression on his face said it all. After a moment, he grinned, acknowledging that Ummer's gentle jibe had hit home. Ummer, for his part, was perhaps the only boy in the dormitory that night who was not swayed by popular opinion. He knew that Afsal had uselessly picked a fight with the jawan.

At the end of each term, Ummer went home for his vacations. Once, in Class VIII, he was heading home for a two-week break. Strangely, not a single bus was plying to Kulgam or Shopian that day. Perplexed, he asked a conductor what was going on.

'There's been a grenade attack on the route between Kulgam and Shopian. The forces are on alert. No bus will go through Kulgam today.'

The conductor banged his hand on the bus door to get the attention of the passengers at the depot. 'Khodwani, Khodwani! Anyone going to Khodwani! This bus is till Khodwani!'

Ummer contemplated this new piece of information. His home was barely an hour on foot from Khodwani! He decided to take the bus instead of heading back to school, as he should have. With a bag on his shoulders and a stick in his hand, he got off at the Khodwani bus stop and started to walk to Kulgam. Midway, he happened to run into a distant cousin who cut off Ummer's warm greeting to ask him where the hell he thought he was headed.

'Home.' Ummer seemed surprised at the question.

'Don't even try going there! The army has cordoned the area. They will definitely arrest you.'

'Why would they arrest me? On what charges? I haven't done anything wrong.'

Despite his cousin's efforts over the next half hour to convince him, Ummer was adamant and resumed his journey home. When he reached the army barricades at Kulgam, a jawan tried to stop him.

'My home is only a little ahead. And I'm a school student. I haven't done anything wrong.'

Ummer tried to free himself from the iron grip of the jawan, who was insisting on checking his bag. He knew now how Afsal must have felt.

'No, no! Don't touch my bag!' he cried. When the jawan couldn't control him any more, he slapped Ummer hard on his face. Reeling from the sheer shock of the assault, Ummer stopped struggling and was dragged inside the camp.

On hearing the commotion, a few senior officers came out of their offices.

'Leave him!' An officer, who seemed to be the one in charge, commanded.

The jawan let go of Ummer immediately.

'We're not here to hurt you. We're here to make sure that no one gets hurt. There are some militants on the loose in the area. They are suspected to be about the same age as you. And we have to make sure that they don't harm anyone. Please let us check your bag,' the officer requested.

Ummer, visibly relaxed since the officer's intervention, was softened by the respect he was now being shown.

'If you don't find anything in my bag, will you let me go?' he demanded.

'Of course.'

'Okay, then. But only if YOU check my bag and not him.'

Ummer pointed at the jawan who had slapped him. The officer asked the man to bring him Ummer's bag. The jawan quickly took this opportunity to have the sniffer dog examine the bag before he brought it to his superior. On opening it, the officer found books, stationery and some clothes. Satisfied, he smiled at Ummer and handed him back his bag.

'What class are you in?'

'Class VIII in JNV, Anantnag,' Ummer said with justifiable pride, as very few got into JNV.

'What do you want to be when you grow up?'

'Someone like you. How can I become like you?' Ummer asked innocently.

'You want to be an army officer?'

'Not just an army officer, but a person like you.'

The officer's conduct had clearly made an impression on Ummer. 'Why, what's special about me?'

'You're not like other army people who beat and torture my friends.'

'How do army people torture your friends?'

'Didn't you see how that jawan treated me?' Ummer said, brazenly pointing at the soldier who had dragged him inside the camp. He wanted to tell him about the 'Islamabad' incident with his friend Afsal in Anantnag, but it was still too soon for him to trust someone from the army that his people had hated for decades. The officer cut the conversation short at that point, but made sure to ask his men to drop Ummer safely to his doorstep.

'No! Please don't send anyone, sir. I'll go on my own.'

Ummer insisted on this, as he knew instinctively that going home by himself was safer for him than being escorted by military personnel. The officer realized the wisdom of the boy's request and complied. Before Ummer left the camp, he said to him, 'If you want to be an officer like me, join the National Defence Academy when you complete your Class XII.' Ummer looked up at the officer, smiled and left for his home.

Jameela, Fayaz, Asmat and Usma were ecstatic to see Ummer, and his ageing grandparents gave thanks to the almighty for one more chance to pamper their only grandson.

'Why can't Sahibji stay with us here?' Grandma Parrey often complained to her daughter-in-law.

'Mouji, let him study well. Only if he makes something of himself will we be able to take you on the Haj. Don't you want to go?' Jameela would reply.

'I don't even know if I will live that long. I'd rather spend time with him now,' the old woman would retort angrily. Little did she know that dying had very little to do with age when it came to her and her grandson.

'Of course you will be. Why do you say such things?' Jameela would reply in a consolatory tone, for she knew her mother-in-law was merely grumpy from constantly missing her grandson.

The grumpy grandmother now walked up to her grandson with a bowl of kheer.

'Do they feed you well in the school, Sahibji?'

'They do, Dadi, but their kheer pales in comparison to yours. I really miss your kheer.'

The vacation flew by. Two days before the start of the following term, Javed came over to Ummer's house.

'Can you tutor me for the test?' Javed had not prepared for the test that was to be conducted on the first day of the new term.

'Why do you always leave things for the last minute, Javed? You should have come earlier.'

'You're the one who does last-minute study. Always. Since the day I met you. If anything, you're to blame for my habit,' Javed retorted playfully.

'That's because when I study, I am all there. Focused on the task. Unlike you, whose mind is always elsewhere.'

At this, Javed got up to wrestle Ummer to the floor and just about succeeded, with his first-mover advantage and also because Ummer was laughing too hard to summon any real strength to resist. Listening to the sound of their banter fill the house, the family was glad that Ummer had Javed for company when he came home from school. However, Fayaz walked in on the wrestling match, frowning.

'Where's the change, Ummer? I think you owe me an account of the money from the grocery expenses?'

Fayaz was meticulous about finances, and ensured that Ummer was also accountable for any money given to him for running household errands. He was careful to teach his son the value of hard-earned money.

That night, as Javed was staying over and because the boys were leaving for school soon, the family table was laden with food that was both abundant and delicious. Teenage stomachs, needless to say, are bottomless pits into which copious amounts of food can disappear without seeming to show up on skinny teenage frames. The boys ate more than they intended to. Barely an hour after the meal, they gently slipped into a sated, coma-like sleep.

It must have been past midnight when someone banged loudly on the Parreys' front door. Fayaz looked through the window and saw half a dozen soldiers at his doorstep. It was a cordon-and-search operation by the army, assisted by the local police and magistrate, to find the boys responsible for blasting grenades on the Kulgam-Shopian road a couple of weeks ago.

Fayaz quickly asked Jameela to confine herself and the other women of the house in a room on the top floor. Then he opened the door, and the soldiers barged in. The family was used to these intrusions by now; this drill was carried out in civilian homes every time there was trouble in the area.

'Who are these boys?' A soldier asked Fayaz, pointing the gun in Ummer and Javed's direction.

'He is my son, and that boy is his friend,' Fayaz specified.

'I've never seen them before. Show me your IDs.'

Ummer and Javed rushed to grab their IDs; they were especially keen on getting the procedure over with before the women of the house were forced to come out in front of the soldiers.

'They study in JNV, Anantnag, and are here for their vacation. Javed, my son's friend, came here this morning. They will both leave for Anantnag day after tomorrow,' Fayaz clarified.

'Come with us!'

The soldiers divided themselves into two groups to search the house thoroughly. One team took Javed, and the other took Ummer. They let the boys lead the entry and search of each room, using them as human shields, for in their experience, militants usually do not kill their own. For the same reason, should the family be harbouring militants, it would be relatively easy to apprehend them as they were less likely to blow up the place. In short, the army was banking on the militants' need for local support.

Javed and Ummer led them through every nook and corner of the house, even the pantry and attic. Half an hour later, they seemed satisfied and left the premises. Afterwards, Fayaz and the boys sat up for a while. Javed was livid; he expressed in no uncertain terms his indignation at the fact that they could walk into the house and conduct a search in the middle of the night. Ummer was quieter, weighing the situation in his mind as he always did. Fayaz said some pertinent things to the boys that night, which swayed his opinion in another direction, in complete contrast to Javed's.

'Due to unfortunate circumstances, the army has been deployed in our state. No doubt, none of this is fair to us. But how is it fair to expect them to do their job without conducting these searches? They have no way of knowing the good from the bad, as many locals are also sympathetic to the militant cause. And it's easier to comb the area at night when the town comes to a standstill. My advice to you boys is, don't bother too much about these things. Just stay focused on your education, and find yourself good jobs eventually. No good ever comes of picking up the gun out of misplaced anger.'

A couple of years later, when Ummer was due to appear for his crucial Class X board exams, the tragic case of Neelofar Jan, aged twenty-two, and her seventeen-year-old sister-in-law, was all over the news. They had gone missing on 29 May 2009 from an apple orchard in Bongam, Shopian. Their mutilated corpses were later discovered in the nearby fields, a kilometre apart. Because the area where the bodies were found was under heavy military surveillance, the locals suspected that the army was responsible for the abduction, rape and murder of the two girls. The army denied all charges and insisted that the young women had drowned in a stream.

Kashmir was burning with anger and erupted in widespread protests overnight. Their collective anguish was apparent in Kulgam, Ganderbal, Anantnag, Bongam, Baramulla, Bandipora and many other districts. The then chief minister ordered a probe into the deaths, and the postmortem confirmed that the women had been gang-raped before they were killed. The younger girl, a bright student, was enrolled in pre-med school. Her pregnant sister-in-law was already the young mother of a two-year-old.

The students at JNV were naturally agitated by the news of this horrific incident. Ummer and Javed were part of many discussions around the topic. They felt the horror of the crime vividly, as the family of those two women could just as well have been theirs. Rahim Iqbal, now in Class XII, was seething with anger and voiced the thoughts of many in the school when he said, 'The Indian Army is evil incarnate. They have been butchering us for years. But the rape of our women is the worst of their crimes. We must take up arms. We must show them what our strength can do.'

Rahim was an intelligent student, a promising sportsman and the son of an affluent family of saffron cultivators. Other students, particularly the juniors, looked up to him, and he had quite a fan club in school. Knowing that he had a captive audience on this occasion, Rahim ranted on.

'Every uniformed man that I see, I will kill. I will use whatever weapon I have. Stones, my bare hands, or Kalashnikovs. Are you all with me on this?' he shouted.

'Yes, we are. Inshallah!' came the strong reply in concurrence.

'We have had enough in Kunan and Pashpora, we will not bear the butchery of our women any longer.'

This proclamation was followed by the chanting of slogans that were popular with old and young alike in Kashmir.

Dil mein rakho Allah ka khauf; hath mein rakho Kalashnikov.
Is paar bhi lenge azadi, uss paar bhi lenge azadi.
Azadi . . . azadi!

Javed was all fired up by the calls for azadi and the mention of Kalashnikovs. It seemed heroic, the mental image of his teenage self brandishing one.

'Isn't this just what we need? We should definitely join him,' whispered Javed.

Javed was rewarded by a resounding smack on the head. Then Ummer turned around and stomped towards the dorm. Sitting on his bed, he fumed at Javed. He just didn't want his closest friend to be drawn into this unsavoury business of militancy. 'We have an exam tomorrow. Study!' he hissed, when Javed came in. Zainub, blissfully unaware of the tension between the two, had finished studying and was fast asleep. Javed had never seen Ummer react like this. All the false bravado he had been feeling just seconds ago quickly evaporated. He sat down sheepishly to study and then suddenly remembered that the school would most likely be closed the next day, what with all the street agitations. And so there would be no exam. He said as much, and this upset and disappointed Ummer even further.

'Education is the only way out for us, Javed. This isn't even politics that we're talking about. We are talking about militancy, about taking on the Indian Army. That will only land us in a coffin. Think about what that would do to our families.'

'You are a coward.'

'If you want to see it that way, so be it. I am only being practical.'

'So what do *you* want to be when you're done with your education?' Javed asked caustically, knowing very well that Ummer hadn't quite made up his mind.

'I think a doctor,' said Ummer, avoiding eye contact as he knew his friend was being mean.

'But you like math, don't you? Then shouldn't you be an engineer?'

'There aren't many job opportunities for engineers here in Kashmir. If I pursue that line, I'll have to move out of here. Honestly, I'm not sure.' Ummer wanted to be an officer like Syed Ata Hasnain, but wasn't sure about telling his friend that for fear of being judged.

'That's true. Most of our seniors, who were any good, left Kashmir. It's no longer a place fit to live,' Javed said, his anger now gone, replaced by heartfelt sympathy for his friend's predicament.

'And you were ready to join the club and add to the madness just a few minutes ago. Pick up a Kalashnikov, was it?' Ummer was now smiling at his friend.

'I'm sorry, but I completely lose it when such atrocities are committed. How can you not react when our women are raped, Ummer? Doesn't your blood boil?'

'Of course, it does! I have two sisters whom I love dearly. But I want to do something with my life that makes a difference, not add to the killings and revenge. History is our best teacher. And the best example I've found so far is Japan. When Hiroshima and Nagasaki were attacked with an atom bomb, they did not react by hurling an atom bomb back at the US. Instead, they focused on redevelopment and replaced the war industries with foreign trade, ship-building and fishing. They put phenomenal hard work into rebuilding their nation. And they took a lot of help and support from the United States!'

'But it was the United States that bombed them!' said Javed, clearly not happy that Japan had taken help from the enemy.

'And what do you think Japan should have done?'

'Bombed them back! An eye for an eye. Fair and square.'

'And then the cycle of destruction would have continued, just like in our Kashmir. The wheel of revenge and avenge needs to be broken, Javed. Those of us who can, should find ways to help. We have to join the system, become the liaison between the state and the people.'

'So what are you going to do?' asked Javed.

Javed seemed to warm up to the idea. He wanted to hear Ummer's opinion and gauge whether there really was a better way to handle the situation. Choices that would help his family and the people of his state.

Ummer didn't reply immediately. He plucked up some courage, took a deep breath and finally said it, 'I know this sounds crazy, but I think I would like to be an army officer.'

Chapter 8

On 15 August 2017, amidst jubilant nation-wide celebrations of the seventieth year of India's independence, I was scheduled to visit Shopian. Kashmir was on high alert at the time as a grenade-lobbing incident had taken place only a few days ago. I came to know about this from Rehman, a junior of Ummer's from school, whom I had tracked down on Facebook. I asked Rehman for his number on Messenger and he was happy to provide it. So we got talking.

After the customary exchanges and respective introductions, we spoke for a while about Ummer. Inevitably, the conversation led to our discussing the current state of affairs in Kashmir.

'Ma'am, the situation in Kashmir is quite tense . . . *yahan ke haalat kharab hain*,' were his exact words. The situation here isn't very good.

'But why?' I believed I knew the answer, but wanted to hear his side of the story.

'Ma'am, today, besides the three necessities—food, clothes and shelter—mobile phones and the Internet have become indispensable. Particularly for the youth, to satisfy their basic social, intellectual and economic needs.

All commercial activities happen on the Internet. But here in Kashmir, connectivity remains suspended for days and sometimes months. I once needed to fill up an application form for a competitive exam. I had to travel to Jammu, complete the form in a cybercafe there, and return to my hometown. An application that would hardly have cost me a few bucks if I had Internet here, cost me four hundred rupees. You can imagine my anger and frustration. Everyone asks us young Kashmiris to do something constructive. How will we do it when we don't have the avenues or the basic facilities?'

Each generation to its own anxiety, I thought. While older Kashmiris worried about peace, azadi and their children dying in a proxy war, here was a youth complaining about Internet connectivity. I imagined that the militants were not affected by it much, but for a young man who wanted to build a peaceful career, it was of vital importance to stay connected to the world at large.

'But why do they turn it off?' I asked, knowing the answer.

'In case of an attack that they call a "terrorist" attack.'

'What do *you* call it?' I adopted a deliberately stern tone.

'I don't know, ma'am.' I could sense the hesitation and uncertainty in his voice, mingled with a desire to convince me. 'Ma'am, why do you think the youth in this place are picking up guns against the system?'

'Maybe because they don't have the Internet?' In that moment, I couldn't think of a more plausible reaction to his question.

'Ma'am, yesterday I had gone to my hometown to meet my family. A CRPF jawan stopped me on the outskirts to check my ID. I've been living in this area ever since I was born, and an outsider who doesn't even know this land has the authority to check my ID. Why?'

Rehman was angry again. I listened to him patiently, even as I wondered how he could tell a CRPF jawan from an army jawan.

'Even I submit to ID checks whenever and wherever it's required, Rehman.'

He didn't seem convinced, 'Not as frequently as we have to. You can't imagine how frustrating it is, not being able to move about freely in your own place. Do you know, our parents don't allow us out of our homes after seven! Even if we go out, we have to make sure that we carry a light with us. If we don't, we get shot at. I suppose you go out for late-night movies or parties sometimes. Does this happen to you in your hometown?'

He was angrier now. Then he mentioned the incident of two teenage boys who were killed by the army on 8 November 2014 in Budgam in a case of mistaken identity.

'Rehman, that vehicle refused to stop at two barriers and tried to break through the third barrier. If they were innocent, they should have stopped at the barrier,' I tried to reason with him.

'The truth is always different from the media version. The media manipulates information. We have no trust in the national media.'

In the absence of trust, a conversation is in danger of turning into a useless argument. Wishing to avoid that at any cost, I let Rehman speak.

'My friend Amir had come home to celebrate Eid. He was only an exam away from getting his MBA degree. And he got shot by the army. Can you imagine the plight of his parents? He was an unarmed civilian. Just a student who wanted to withdraw money from an ATM to deposit his fees, and they gunned him down.' Rehman's voice trembled, and for a moment he could barely speak. 'I've lost too many friends, ma'am. They didn't even spare the one who joined the army and who was on their side.'

He was now referring to Ummer and the Indian Army. I could relate to his despair. There can be nothing worse than living in a place where young men die uselessly in the name of a war that will not end unless one side is annihilated completely. Human life has little value in India in the present scheme of things, I mused, and even less in Kashmir.

Rehman spoke after a long pause, 'I have four brothers; the oldest is a PhD, but none of them have jobs. We're all sitting at home, useless, with no scope for employment anywhere. The government doesn't know what we want or need. They have to send interlocutors from India to find that out? Has anyone really ever tried to speak to us—we, the people of Kashmir?'

I continued to listen to him patiently. He had lost friends whom he loved, and I didn't want to be insensitive.

'It was all over the news that Sonu Nigam's morning sleep gets disturbed by the call of the azaan. Can you imagine our plight when the armed forces come knocking on our doors in the middle of the night for a search operation? It's like an everyday affair! They wake up men, women and even children. Everybody was concerned about Sonu Nigam's sleep. What about our sleep, ma'am?'

'Then why do you let armed militants into your houses? Why don't you report them to the police or the army?' I shot back.

'First of all, they are our people. Secondly, they never misbehave like the army does. And thirdly, if we don't let them in, they will kill us, and who wants to die, ma'am?'

'Do you realize that these militants possess weapons illegally?'

'That's more dangerous for us than for the army, ma'am. We are threatened from both sides, but at least the militants don't misbehave with us.'

'Of course. They only kill.' I couldn't hold back my sarcasm, but felt guilty at the same time. 'Do YOU also want azadi, Rehman?'

'What I want doesn't matter.'

Sadly, this was true. Rehman was an inconsequential entity in a big, inhuman power game that seemed to have no end. I genuinely felt sorry for boys like him. They were faced, as he told me, with a difficult choice: leave the Valley, make a career outside Kashmir and never look back, or be absorbed into the vicious cycle of a proxy war.

'But for how long can I stay away from my land and why should I? I love Kashmir, and I really want the situation to improve.'

I knew Rehman's was the voice of many a young man or woman from the Valley, but also realized the futility of continuing in this vein and tried to change the topic.

'I'll be visiting your school soon. Can you put me in touch with Ummer's teachers?'

'Most of them have been transferred, but there are some you can talk to. I'll let them know you're going there, and also pass on their phone numbers to you. Where will you be staying?'

'I'll be staying in an army camp. There are no hotels there,' I clarified, an apologetic explanation that I would find myself giving to many Kashmiris in the future, lest they judge me and withhold vital information.

'So it's Aishmuqam! 3 RR.'

'How do you know?'

'Our school comes under them, ma'am. It's not far from the school. Hope I see you there, but in case I can't make it, I wish you all the best with my friend's story. He was a brave boy. I only have one request.'

'What might that be?'

'Please write the truth,' he pleaded.

'Truth is like love, Rehman. Everybody has their version of it. Thank you for telling me yours. I'll try to do justice to your friend, that I can assure you.'

With that promise, I ended my conversation with Rehman.

Now my destination was Jawahar Navodaya Vidyalaya in Aishmuqam, Anantnag. I had rescheduled my Independence Day flight to Srinagar for 17 August, owing to security reasons cited by the commanding officers in Anantnag. But on the 17th, I was terribly late for unexplainable reasons and would have missed the flight if it weren't for a kind ground crew worker at the airport. He spoke to the pilot and persuaded him to let me get on the flight after all my requests had failed and, like a stubborn kid in a toy shop, I had no option but to throw tantrums. My saviour from the ground staff instructed me to board the aircraft without my luggage, promising to send it on the same flight the next day. On second thoughts, the man probably helped me board that flight out of sheer embarrassment at my behaviour and was glad to be finally rid of me.

The moment I was seated in the plane, I received a call from Major Ajay in Aishmuqam.

'Ma'am, have you boarded the flight?'

'Yes, I have,' I said, with a false sense of achievement.

'Ma'am, please switch off your mobile. We are about to take off,' the airhostess interrupted. I begged for an extra minute, and continued talking like a typically irritating passenger.

'So you don't even have clothes?' the major asked incredulously, when I explained that I had been compelled to leave my luggage behind. I was speechless, as I had actually not thought about this until he brought it up. I could swear I heard a chuckle at the other end of the line, before Major Ajay said, 'Don't worry ma'am, just come and we will manage something. I'm glad that you could make it, else reorganizing your visit to the school would have taken even more time.' So my boarding fiasco had been well worth the embarrassment it had caused me!

On reaching Aishmuqam, I was welcomed by Major Ajay who was organizing my visit to the school. After dinner, I was given a clean but oversized tracksuit that probably belonged to one of the officers in the camp. Although I studiously avoided looking in the mirror that day, I couldn't help but see the suppressed hilarity on the faces of everyone who set their eyes on me.

The next day, I was advised by the camp's CO, Colonel C.P. Singh, to give a lecture to the students at the school.

'Ma'am, we hear you give motivational talks. You've come so far to visit the school, why deny these students an opportunity to learn from you?'

I thought the colonel had a point. Besides, the talk could be a means of befriending the kids and getting them to talk in a friendly, relaxed environment.

Although the school wasn't far from the camp, I was informed that no local transport was available. So I got into the army vehicle that was arranged for me, and was perplexed to see a security group occupy the front and back seats immediately. Overwhelmed, I asked Colonel C.P. Singh if a military escort wasn't a little excessive under the circumstances.

'Ma'am, it's not just for you, but also for my driver and the vehicle that is carrying you. Army vehicles and convoys are extremely vulnerable in this area.'

On reaching the school, I asked the security group to leave as I could sense that the students would be uncomfortable in their presence. I didn't want to risk destroying my rapport with them before I had even started building it.

My audience at JNV that day was a batch of Class XII students. Having delivered many motivational lectures to children of this age group elsewhere, I was pretty confident when I walked into that classroom. The moment I entered, amidst their formal greetings, I could feel the pulse of the group. They were eager to find out what I had to offer, of course, but above all, they were anxious to know if I was on their side. And if not, could they get me on their side? As teachers, we learn the art of positive manipulation early in our careers. It helps break the ice with students, and when they believe that you're on their team, they listen more attentively. I played this part to perfection.

After showing them a few motivational videos, I encouraged them to speak about their goals by asking, 'What do you want to become when you grow up?' I started with the girls, dressed in white salwar kameez with hijabs covering their heads. Some said 'doctor', a few wanted to become administrative officers, and many were clueless. I had the impression that several of them said something, anything, only because I was asking.

When I asked the boys, they appeared even more clueless than the girls. Just to lighten the moment and stimulate some conversation, I made an impulsive statement that I regretted immediately afterwards, 'I hope you don't want to become stone-pelters!'

There was an eerie silence in the room; no one uttered a word in response. The confidence I had built till then, using a careful selection of videos and anecdotes, seemed to vanish into thin air. Sighing inwardly, I started the process of rapport-building again from scratch, with less hopes of success this time.

There was one boy who came up with an unusual answer to the vocational question, 'Ma'am, I want to be an interlocutor between India and Pakistan.' Now this was a response I'd never come across in my entire career as a career trainer!

'That's wonderful. And what will you do?' I asked.

'I'll tell them that peace, and not war, is the solution in the long run.'

The other students seemed to look at him with disdain. I had planned to avoid discussing politics with the students. It was a reluctance that probably reflected the national habit of hushing meaningful debates by sweeping sensitive issues under the carpet. But then I realized that the children gathered in the classroom that day represented both the future of Kashmir and the possibility of change. They were at an age where they were vulnerable and yet full of energy. While the youth of other states were picking up books or tools, some of them were forced to pick up guns and stones. I wanted to know what was going on in their minds. Concluding my motivational lecture with an inspiring video, I asked the children if they had any questions for me.

'Why are you here, ma'am, and where are you from?' A boy asked me.

'I'm from Punjab and I'm writing a book on your senior, Lieutenant Ummer Fayaz. Did you know him?' I deliberately mentioned the rank, as a gesture of respect to Ummer in front of his juniors. But I soon realized it didn't matter at all to any of them.

'Yes ma'am, he was our senior.' Some boys spoke up. While the boys were interacting with me, the girls were invariably quiet, I observed.

'Would you want to be like Lieutenant Ummer Fayaz?' I asked, recollecting that most of them didn't want to join the army.

'No, ma'am,' they chorused in low voices.

I blinked and shook my head. 'Why?'

'Because he joined the army, society here did not accept him.'

Yes! There were some who didn't consider his death to be of any value and some who didn't consider him a true Kashmiri.

Just then, the bell rang to signal that the period allotted to me was over. I made haste to ask the staff coordinator, G.N. Rather, for some more time with the students. I told him I wanted to talk to the children who knew Ummer and had spent some time with him in his schooldays. Rather was one of the most senior teachers in JNV school, and granted my request immediately.

'No problem, ma'am, you could take the students to the principal's room so that we can use this room for regular classes.'

'I'd be thankful to anyone who would like to sit with me and tell me more about Ummer.'

I made the announcement and left for the principal's office. It was empty as the principal was out on a visit. I wasn't really expecting any of the students to come, but to my surprise, the whole class came out to talk to me.

I sat on a chair and the students settled down on the carpeted floor. 'You can remove your shoes if you want.'

The moment I said this, all the girls said, 'No', in sync, clinching their noses with their fingers.

'Ma'am, their feet will stink.' They were referring to the boys. The room filled with laughter. I was finally at ease, as the students now seemed to feel comfortable with me. The principal's absence also made a crucial difference, of course.

'So what can you tell me about Ummer?' I started the conversation.

'He shouldn't have joined the army, ma'am. Society here doesn't like the army.' A boy spoke up.

Ummer celebrates Holi at the NDA with his coursemates

Ummer with a coursemate at the NDA

The author with Ummer's mother and father

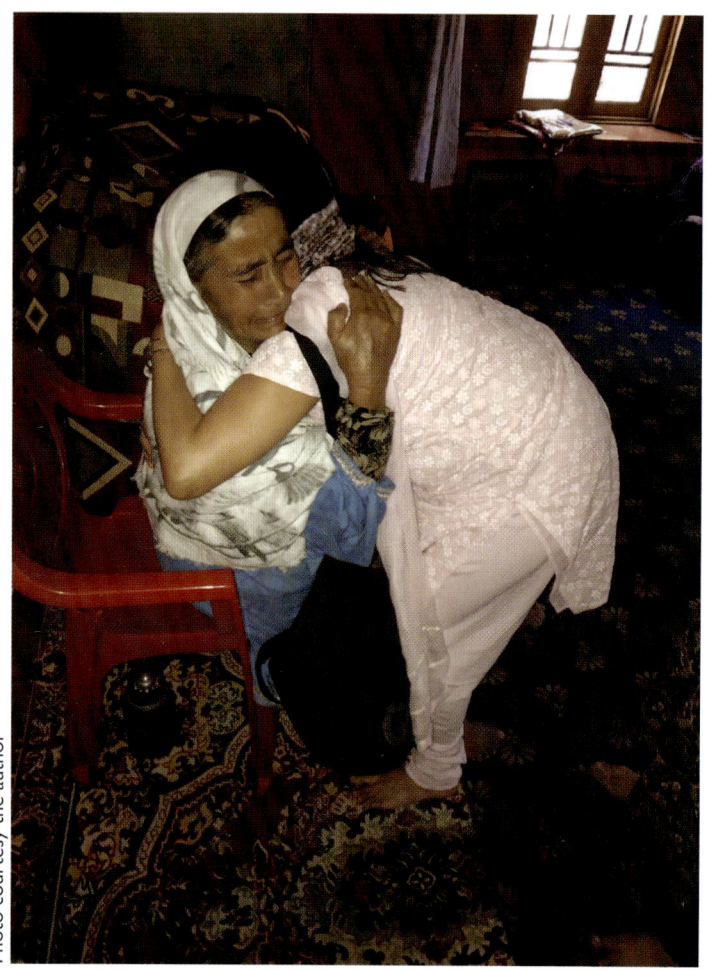

The author with Ummer's grandmother, who was crying inconsolably and saying, 'Ummer loved kheer.'

The author conducting a motivational talk and career counselling session for Ummer's juniors at Jawahar Navodaya Vidyalaya (JNV) School, Anantnag, as part of the army's Sadbhavana project

The house from where Ummer was kidnapped

Ummer's bust at the IMA

Ummer's room at the IMA

Donation to 2 Raj Rif for setting up an award for meritorious students from JNV, Anantnag, Ummer's school. The royalties from this book are being donated to this fund by the author

'Of course, the army killed him because he was a Kashmiri.' Another boy reasoned.

It was hard for me, coming from a background that revered the army, to digest the fact that these youngsters could have such a negative opinion of our armed forces.

'There are so many Kashmiris in the army. Do you think the army will kill them all?' I retorted, pointing out the hole in his argument.

'You don't know what the army does here, ma'am!'

'Tell me. I want to know.'

The students had seen me arrive with a military escort, and hence were a little apprehensive about speaking freely. So I broke the ice by telling them what I knew about Ummer, and how I had gone about my research so far. Slowly, they warmed to the topic and got into a conversation with me.

One of the boys asked me, 'Why do you think Ummer joined the army? Was it by choice or by chance?'

I admitted that I really didn't know, so the boy unfolded it for me by revealing that he had met Ummer once after he had joined the army, and asked him the same question.

'He said that it was just a matter of chance that he joined the army, but later it became a choice.'

I was truly happy to hear that because I happen to believe that even if a boy lands up in a military academy by chance, he should come out of it with the army as his first choice, or the very purpose of training is defeated.

Another boy shot a question at me, 'Ma'am, why are you writing a book on Ummer Fayaz? He is not of much importance here.'

'Then whom should I write a book on?' I didn't bother to conceal my sarcasm.

'Ma'am, you should write a book on our hero!'

'And who is that, if I may ask?'

'Burhan Wani. And your book will get full media attention too.'

I could only smile in the face of what the audience in front of me probably thought of as foolishness.

'And who will give me the information on him?'

'We will, ma'am. We will take you to his house.'

'What if his parents don't entertain me?'

'They will make you sit and give you tea. They will be pleased to know that someone is writing a book on their son. After all, he sacrificed his life for us. Ummer didn't do anything like that.'

No matter how eager the students and Burhan Wani's parents were for me to write a book showcasing him as a hero, I'll be honest in saying that my idea of heroism was different. Why should a terrorist's family be given so much importance?

'But Burhan Wani was a terrorist,' I said plainly.

'Why do you call him a terrorist, ma'am? He was our patriot, the way Bhagat Singh was yours!'

They had me at that, and I abandoned the argument. Some things, sometimes, are best left unreasoned.

'Did you hear about Kunan Poshpora, the lynching of Muslims who eat beef, the Neelofar Jan rape case? These incidents are etched in the memory of every Kashmiri and have led to the demand for azadi. We will not give up till we get it.'

They stamped the conversation with their intent, underlining their statements with slogans. I, on the other hand, was clearly avoiding conflict, so as to let them articulate their thoughts and express themselves freely. Consequently, my responses were little more than mild crackers to their atom bombs.

'But why are you so angry with the army?'

'Ma'am, you were talking about stone-pelters! Do you know why stones are thrown at the army?'

'Why?'

'The army still has some sense. They don't mess with us unless necessary. But the police, CRPF and BSF, they keep checking our identity cards. They stop us anywhere and question us. We are only students, ma'am.'

I was thinking of the sheer hard work and restraint the Indian Army had shown, and the lives it must have given, to earn that opinion from a local boy.

'Only yesterday he got arrested.' Another boy said, pointing at the boy sitting next to him. I asked why.

'Ma'am, they were troubling him during an identity card check, and when he protested, they put him in jail. His father had to come and get him released.'

I refused to sympathize with that story, convinced that the boy had misbehaved in some way.

'I don't believe this. In any case, you could have just shown your ID and gotten away without all this drama.'

'Why should we prove our identity in our own land? Do you also do this in Punjab?' The boy who had been arrested demanded.

'Yes, if there is an inspection, I always stop to show my driving licence, which happens to be an ID card.'

'But not every day, ma'am. We have to do this every day. They raid our homes in the middle of the night to conduct searches. All that they find are our women sleeping with small children. Do you think it's a noble gesture to barge into someone's house like that? Don't Kashmiris have a right to privacy?'

The boy's complaints had risen to a shrill pitch, and when he heard that himself, he kept quiet for a brief moment before continuing, 'I will fight till the day I don't have to show my identity card in my own land.' He finally stopped talking, at the sight of my face that showed emotions of surprise, sympathy, helplessness and fear, all at once.

I wanted to tell him that there are no terrorists in Punjab any more who blow people up in the name of freedom, self-determination or faith. I wanted to tell him that I sleep peacefully in my home because no militants come to my house asking for shelter. I wanted to tell him about Punjab's lost generation, lost before the political powers decided to end terrorism once and for all. I wanted to say so much more to those students, but ended up telling them only one thing.

'I think you should all study and make a career for yourselves that you can bank on. If you fight guns with guns, you'll only end up dead. If you're peaceful and if you stop protesting, the army will have no reason to be here. Someone has to start.'

They spoke to me about everything from Gaza and Palestine to Yemen and Iraq and Syria and Bangladesh, about the cruelties inflicted on Muslims everywhere in the world. As I thought to myself about what they were saying, I remembered the many arguments that I had heard about these issues.

Some were quite clear that everywhere, Muslims had first created a problem and when the situation got out of hand and governments intervened, they played victim. They felt that peaceful co-existence was an alien word to many from that religion and many from that religion who want peace suffer due to others. They talked about many incidents of terrorism and felt that when history keeps repeating itself with legitimate evidence, then one is forced to think ill of the religion.

Others felt differently. They felt that not everyone was bad and things couldn't be generalized. This was a never-ending argument.

At this point, the bell rang again, and the students had to disperse for their midday meal. However, they asked me to join them for lunch, determined to convince me that they were victimized in every possible way. That wasn't the first time I was encountering such a bid for sympathy in Kashmir.

Rather came into the office, and asked me about the interaction. I gave him a brief overview, and then made a call to the army camp to coordinate my return. Meanwhile, the students gave their teacher some feedback about the discussion. He listened to them patiently and then instructed them to go to the dining hall.

'So ma'am, what do you think about our students?' Rather asked with some pride, when I had finished my phone call.

'I think they're all very bright and have a great future ahead of them if they're guided properly.' I added, 'They seemed angry, though, and carry a lot of baggage that isn't even theirs. Some of the incidents they mentioned happened decades ago. I think it's time to move on, and work towards building good careers rather than holding grudges or seeking revenge.'

'See ma'am, in all fairness, we are the ones who are getting cheated. The government now wants to challenge Article 35A and Article 370.*'

'But don't you think that the articles are actually working against the development of your state in the present scenario?'

'Who says? These are special privileges that have been given to us. Why should we let them go? It's not fair.'

I wondered at the fact that the teacher was for the two articles. Sometimes, I reflected, you have enjoyed a privilege for so long that you don't realize when it actually starts working against you.

Rather then asked the girl students to escort me to the dining hall for lunch. Humbled, I thanked him.

'Ma'am, please enjoy our hospitality, whatever little we can offer. In fact, you should have stayed here in our guest house so that we could have looked after you better.'

'I'm sorry, sir, I didn't know that you had guest rooms here. Maybe next time I'll plan things better.'

'If you're here tomorrow, then we can help you shift, send a vehicle to carry your luggage.'

'It's just a day, sir, and I'm already settled at the camp. Next time for sure.'

---

* Article 35A of the Indian Constitution is a section that empowers the Jammu and Kashmir state legislature to define 'permanent residents' of the state and provide special rights and privileges to those permanent residents. Article 370 of the Indian Constitution conferred on Jammu and Kashmir the power to have a separate constitution, a state flag and autonomy of internal administration. On 5 August 2019, the Government of India abrogated Article 370 through a Presidential Order and a parliamentary resolution.

I walked with the girls to the dining hall; they seemed excited at the opportunity for some exclusive conversation with me, uninterrupted by the boys.

'Ma'am, are all women in your place as confident and intelligent as you?' One of the girls ventured to ask.

'You don't have confident and intelligent women in Kashmir?'

'There are very few, ma'am, because we don't get many opportunities.'

'The situation is the same everywhere, but when you don't get an opportunity, you create one.' I smiled at her.

We sat on a wooden bench at a wooden table. A mess worker served me some food, and I ate with the girls. I looked around the dining hall, thinking in my head that Ummer must have eaten in the same hall for many years before he joined the National Defence Academy (NDA) in Pune.

For some reason, the girls seemed to admire me, and this made me smile. One girl with naughty eyes wanted to know, 'Do you have a boyfriend, ma'am?'

I blushed but didn't want to spoil the image I'd projected of being a strong, independent woman, so I said, 'I did. But we broke up.'

'Do you have his picture?' I could see that the girls were expecting me to show them a picture of my ex-boyfriend.

'No, I don't.' They seemed so disappointed that I quickly said, 'I may have it on Facebook. Let me check.'

Their eyes shone with anticipation as I scrolled down my phone. When I showed them a picture, they snatched the phone from me and later from each other to take a good look.

'He is handsome,' was the verdict, as they handed my phone back to me.

'Why didn't you marry him, ma'am? He seems like a handsome boy.'

I smiled mysteriously, and diverted the conversation by asking them questions.

'So how are girls treated in you families?' I wanted to know more about the girls in the Valley these days, and also whether Ummer had a girlfriend.

'It's better to have a girl in the house today, ma'am, because most boys either take the path of jihad and never return to the family, or get shot down by the forces.' A grim situation indeed, I thought.

'Do soldiers misbehave with students?' I wanted to hear their account of it.

'Ma'am, when the people you call "militants" come to our house ...'

Another girl nudged her, gesturing to her to be quiet, and she just trimmed her answer to, 'Not all of them, ma'am. Some do it only as a part of their job or because it's their nature.'

'Did Ummer have a girlfriend?' I thought I could ask that question since they had asked me about my boyfriend and I had been honest about it.

'We were very young when Ummer was in school, but all the girls loved him. He was like the school hero. We always knew that he would do something big in life. But unfortunately, we lost him. People must have killed him out of jealousy only because all the girls loved him,' the same girl said sadly.

'You must have seen that the boys here are quite useless. They don't think rationally. Ummer was different. He never took part in radical talk. All he wanted was to make something of himself so that he could help his people. He did have a girlfriend, her name is Tahzun,' another girl in the group told me.

I wanted to know more, but they refused to divulge any more details. The people of Kashmir, I realized, had been trained a little too well to keep secrets. No matter how hard you tried, the locals who wanted a peaceful life would never talk about the militants or about the forces. If they supported one, the other would become their enemy. Yet, taking a side was important, as one couldn't afford to make enemies out of both. But when it came to making a choice, it was always better to support your own people. That was the predicament of being a Kashmiri.

Chapter 9

Destiny was, quietly, bringing new people into Ummer's life, those who would transform the course of his life forever.

Ummer was now attending JNV, Ganderbal, as his entire class had been transferred there. With continuous strife in Kashmir, schools had a shortage of staff, as the teachers could not commute. Hence, Ummer's batch of Class XI was transferred to JNV, Ganderbal, while Class X and Class XII batches were transferred to JNV, Ferozepur, so that the students' education did not suffer.

Witty, energetic and dedicated to learning, Ummer made his presence felt in the new school almost immediately. The staff adored him and he had quite the fan base among his juniors as well.

Saturday nights were movie nights in JNV. One particular weekend, they played the DVD of a Shah Rukh Khan starrer, *My Name is Khan*, and the students went to bed excited, with the raw performance of Shah Rukh imprinted on their minds. The next morning, a few of them hatched a plan to persuade the warden to screen another blockbuster, *Dabangg*, starring Salman Khan, on Sunday night. But their weekly movie allowance was restricted to Saturdays and they knew they wouldn't be granted another movie night during the same weekend. Unless, maybe, if Ummer asked.

'With an exam on Monday, you guys want to watch *Dabangg* tonight? And you want me to go do the asking?'

'It's Salman Khan! Which world do you live in that he has no effect on you! And don't give us the good cop advice. If it had been a cricket match, you would have already asked them by now and sat up all night to watch too!' Javed chided.

Tahzun, two years younger than Ummer, pleaded softly, 'Please just ask the warden for the TV room keys. He'll give them only to you.'

Ummer couldn't help smiling at her, or melting at the sheer desperation in her voice. 'Fine! I'll go ask and take my chances. But if he says no, I can't be held responsible.'

Javed trotted beside him on the way to the warden's room. 'So I ask you and you remind me about studying, but a girl asks you and you agree, almost immediately? Nice!' he teased.

Ummer gave him a friendly cuff on the head, but grinned impishly. 'Why are you so hung up on Salman Khan anyway? You're just as handsome. Besides, all you have to do is conjure up Salman and he'll write your exam for you,' Ummer quipped affectionately.

Thanks to Ummer, Javed and the others got to watch movies on two consecutive nights and were hypnotized for three dazzling hours. However, the fantasy spell was shattered by the exam the next day. Javed almost had a cardiac arrest when he looked at the question paper. 'I don't know the answers to any of these questions. Help me,' he hissed at Ummer, who rolled his eyes. He had known this was coming. He swiftly wrote the answers to a few questions on an extra sheet and handed it over to Javed. But after the exam, Ummer grilled his friend for hours, tutoring him on the entire syllabus all over again. He even prepared mock exams, and made Javed redo them until he was sure that he got most of them correct.

Tahzun noticed Ummer's concern for his friend; it was one of the reasons she liked him instantly. But she wasn't alone in her admiration. There was a fleet of girls in school who had their first crush on Ummer. But it must be true that one doesn't go looking for love. Love finds you. Especially in the case of someone like Ummer, whose relationships were deeper and more selfless than the average.

It all started with the chaos of the Anantnag students joining the JNV branch at Ganderbal midway through the year, stretching school resources pretty thin. There were never enough plates to go around at lunchtime. So the girls ate first and then the boys. Fed up of waiting for the staff to find them plates, Ummer decided one day to just ask the girls for one himself. He happened to walk straight up to Tahzun, who flushed crimson at his request but happily gave him her plate from which she had eaten earlier. She was hustled out of the mess that day by her friends, who teased her mercilessly.

'Ah, so he wants to eat out of your plate,' said one jealous voice.

'How come he asked you? Does he know you?' said another.

The fact that Ummer seemed completely oblivious to all this female attention only added to his charm. And so he thought nothing of walking up to Tahzun each day, to ask for her plate. It became a regular habit, and soon it was Tahzun who would wait for Ummer to show up so that she could offer him her plate. One day, he didn't turn up for lunch, and Tahzun found herself terribly distraught, to the extent that the shy girl mustered the courage to walk up to Javed and ask why Ummer had not come. Javed informed her that his friend had gone for a chess tournament and would only return in the evening. At the time, Ummer was a national-level chess player, training for national-level school games organized by the School Games Federation of India.

At dinner that night, the boys, being boys, were all discussing the girl who had a crush on Ummer.

'I think there's a girl who likes you and wants to come tell you about it,' Javed said slyly.

'Oh yeah? Who is she?' said Ummer, sounding nonchalant as he mixed some rice and dal on his plate. Ummer loved rice, and this was his favourite meal.

'I'm not sure either. There were some guys talking about it and I overheard. It could be the girl who asked me about you at lunch. The same girl you've been taking your lunch plate from. Tahzun?'

'I take the plate from her because she sits in the corner of the first row. It's more convenient than walking around to the other end to ask another girl. Besides, she's always still eating when I come, unlike the other girls who finish early and leave the mess,' shrugged Ummer, careful not to give his feelings away.

'So it doesn't make you wonder why she's still sitting there so late while all the other girls have left?'

Ummer got up to place his plate at the 'Used' counter but Javed wouldn't let him get away with it.

'You like her too!' he shrieked.

'Why are you bothering me about this?' said an irritated Ummer. Javed decided to change tactics.

'How can you not see how difficult it is to be your best friend? You are the most popular guy in school, and so full of yourself that you can't see how hard it is for me,' moaned Javed, bringing out his trump card, a bid for Ummer's sympathy. His histrionics had the desired effect on Ummer, who mellowed immediately.

'Honestly, I haven't really spoken to her except for the plate exchanges. I hardly know who she is. But we can find out,' he said with a wink.

Ummer was quick to sense the insecurity behind his friend's teasing manner. In fact, he wasn't completely blind to the attention he received from the opposite sex, but only because he noticed that it seemed to bother Javed sometimes. The girls often struck up a conversation with Javed in the hope of hanging out with Ummer or learning more about him. Javed, on the other hand, had learnt to circumvent his insecurity by using his friend's popularity to his own advantage. So he often strutted around campus, toting Ummer as a sort of prized trophy. The dynamics of friendship are indeed complex!

Meanwhile, Ummer continued to observe Tahzun during their breaks, and while her friends began to say hi to him, both Ummer and Tahzun refrained from initiating any pleasantries. The entire year passed thus, and neither expressed their feelings for the other.

In many ways, Tahzun and Ummer had very similar backgrounds. Both hailed from lower middle-class families, and had fathers who had worked very hard to bring up their children. Both understood, at a very young age, the value of money, a good education and hard work. And yet, their dissimilarities had seemingly brought them together, in a classic case of attraction of opposites. Tahzun was introverted and unassuming, while Ummer was outgoing, though not in a boisterous way. And so their love unfolded. Clumsily, in the way that it often does with teenagers. Subtly, in keeping with their gentle personalities. And magically, before they even knew it themselves.

At the end of the year, Ummer and his classmates had to return to Anantnag. All the anxiety that had accompanied their move to Ganderbal only a few months earlier seemed unfounded. They were now experiencing immense sadness at the thought of leaving their new friends behind.

Tahzun for one was going through far greater turmoil than all her friends put together. She was sad that Ummer was leaving, but her grief was intensified by the thought that she had not let him know how she felt. The other girls were feeling rather giddy with all the emotion in the air, and decided that they wanted the boys, and Ummer in particular, to write in their slam books. Tahzun, feeling too shy to go herself, sent her slam book with her friend. But Ummer refused to write in it.

Tahzun took this as some sort of rejection and cried her eyes out. She skipped dinner that night.

Ummer waited a long time for her and finally got a plate from someone else. But he was uneasy and couldn't resist asking Rehmat, Tahzun's friend, where she was. Loyal to her friend but suddenly hopeful that she was wrong about the rejection, she told Ummer in no uncertain terms that he had hurt Tahzun.

'You refused to write a message in her slam book!' she said accusingly.

'Oh that! I just thought that if someone really wanted an autograph, then they should come themselves. And I had no idea it was hers,' he lied.

In reality, Ummer had wanted Tahzun to come herself so that he could meet her. Clearly, the plan had backfired. And just like that, it slowly dawned on Ummer, that it hurt him to have hurt her. He sat down to think about it and wondered why his heart was churning if it had all just been about sharing a plate with Tahzun. Either way, he knew that he had to make it up to her. So he walked right up to Tahzun when he saw her again the next day.

'Hello, I'm Ummer,' he introduced himself awkwardly, his hand outstretched for a handshake.

Tahzun was in no mood to make this easy for him and, ignoring the offered hand, gave him a terse 'I know' in reply.

'You're Tahzun, right? I've been getting your plate almost every day, but we never got to be friends. I just thought that was odd and wanted to break the ice.'

Tahzun listened intently now, but still didn't want to relent.

'Oh, could I also please write in your slam book? Yesterday, I didn't know it was yours. Do you have it with you today?'

At that, Tahzun felt that fresh salt was being sprinkled on her wounds, reminding her of yesterday's slight. She just got up and walked away.

Ummer sighed, realizing this probably wasn't an issue he could solve with straight talk. He went to Javed for advice. Javed put it plain and square.

'You should have spoken to her a long time ago. But better late than never. And from what I'm seeing, you definitely have a crush on her.'

Javed wasn't helping at all. Ummer stared at his friend in frustration for a moment or two. Then he sat down and penned a long note, guarding it zealously from Javed's inquisitive eyes. Having rolled the paper up and tied some string around it, he appealed to Javed to help him plant the note in Tahzun's school bag.

'There is no way I am standing here all day waiting for them to leave class so we can slip this in her bag,' Javed hissed.

'So let's ask her friend Rehmat when they have a games or music class. That way we know for sure when they will leave the classroom,' Ummer countered. He was determined to find a way to get the note to Tahzun.

Finally, the duo did the deed and waited impatiently for lunch. Ummer made sure to go in a little late and his heart started to sing as soon as he entered the mess and set his eyes on Tahzun. For she was smiling at him. Ecstatic that his note had cleared up the misunderstanding, Ummer walked up to her, smiling back.

After a few moments of awkward talk, Ummer said, 'Today is my last day in Ganderbal. I hope we can continue being friends and stay in touch?'

Tahzun nodded shyly. That one meeting was enough to clinch the deal for both of them. They would speak to each other on the phone often, long after Ummer left Ganderbal.

Just before the Class XII board exams, Ummer vigorously enrolled himself for all the competitive examinations that were to follow, except for the medical entrance. Around this time, a team of counsellors from the army came to the school for campus recruitment to the army as well as to provide motivational orientation for other professional careers. They were part of what is called the Perception Management Programme, intended to win the locals over to a more positive perception of the armed forces and to direct the youth towards more productive goals.

Ummer was suddenly reminded of the inspiring officer in Kulgam who had treated him with such respect while checking his ID on the day of the grenade attack back when he was in Class VIII. He filled up the forms for the NDA, not really knowing at that point what the army could offer him as an employer. It was simply yet another exam that he had to clear.

With a mountain range of entrance exams looming over him, Ummer moved to Srinagar to get some coaching. Throughout this time, he was in touch with Tahzun. He shared all his hopes and ambitions with her, plotting and re-plotting his plans. Tahzun wasn't particularly thrilled about the NDA because Kashmiris in general don't really like people from the army or police cadres. Growing up in the Valley, she had seen how lives were snuffed out every day. Innocent lives were often collateral damage in encounters and counter-encounters between the army and the militants.

But Ummer convinced her, saying, 'If I can't fight for myself, how will I fight for you, should the need arise? This decision should not be influenced by common perception.'

Tahzun was more inclined towards the air force for Ummer. She persuaded him that fighter pilots were the most glamorous with their uniforms and their big birds up in the skies only because she didn't want Ummer to wear an army uniform.

'Okay, I'll join the air force then,' Ummer said. He was deeply in love with Tahzun and knew that she only wanted the best for him. However, the deal was that he would sit for all the entrance exams. At that age, Tahzun was any day a bigger motivation than any army officer for Ummer and that much of a bargain was reasonable.

It was April 2012. Militants with grenades attacked Humhama on the outskirts of Srinagar. Although no lives were lost, Internet services were shut down for several days as part of security measures. Ummer needed to fill up his NDA form and his habit of leaving things for the last minute cost him dearly this time, leaving him no other option but to travel all the way to Jammu to complete the application online. The trip cost him four hundred rupees. Two hours after he got back, the Internet came back on in Srinagar. He was stumped by the irony of it, but relieved that he had sent in his form on time.

The unexpected journey to Jammu had done him out of money for the rest of the month. And while he was generally prudent, there was one expense he just could not avoid. He needed money to recharge his prepaid mobile so that he could call Tahzun. Since they last spoke, he knew that she would be worried. The Internet shutdown and his sudden trip to Jammu just after the grenade attack must have compounded her anxiety.

For Asmat and Usma, their brother was their world.

'Bhaiya, why do you leave everything for the last moment?' Usma admonished her big brother. 'If you had filled the form on time, you could have avoided travelling in such a volatile situation. And spared us the tense moments too.'

Ummer, ever optimistic but feeling the pulse of his sister, pacified her by saying, 'When I make something of myself, all my money will belong to you and Asmat.'

'Nice of you to say, but that wasn't the point at all. It was about doing things on time so you wouldn't put yourself in danger,' Usma shot back.

Ummer smiled because he knew she was right. He kissed her on the forehead, and headed out to recharge his phone and call Tahzun.

'Yes, yes, I did put air force down as my first choice,' he assured Tahzun. 'When I get through, I will fly you out of here with me forever.'

Tahzun was touched by the idealistic yet wistful tone of his voice. When the results came out in October, Ummer's family was jubilant.

Just about every child of Ummer's age in the vicinity had appeared for the entrance exams, but he was the only one to clear each and every one of them! He now had to choose between all the engineering exams that he had cleared and the NDA exam conducted by the Union Public Service Commission (UPSC).

The next step in the NDA programme was an interview at the SSB, Allahabad, also infamously known as the rejection centre because most candidates don't make it past this round. To attend this interview, Ummer had to travel outside Kashmir for the first time in his life. A bus to Srinagar and a train from there to Allahabad brought him to his destination. He couldn't help but notice how beautiful Kashmir was compared to what he saw beyond its borders.

The initial rounds at SSB involved psychological tests, group discussions and ground tasks. Ummer did well in all these rounds. During the personal interview, he became painfully conscious of his Kashmiri-accented English and lack of exposure to the world. While struggling to explain his points of view to the interviewers, he realized that his communication skills could do with a lot of improvement. He was then asked about his relatively poor performance in Class XII compared to his Class X results. His response was heartfelt and spontaneous.

'Sir, where I come from, the schools remain shut for months together. Staff are often on strike. Once, my entire school shut down and we had to relocate to another school with new teachers and an entirely different campus. Even to complete the NDA application, it took me twenty hours' travel to Jammu just to fill up the form. The entire situation is set up to make us lose. So it's a wonder that most of us even graduate.'

Ummer was dejected after the interview; he felt, in hindsight, that his honesty had been unwarranted. He told his father over a call that the truth may not have gone down well with the interviewers.

But to Ummer's surprise, he made it and was asked to report to Varanasi from Allahabad for the Pilot Aptitude Battery Test (PABT) for selection to the air force.

There were other candidates who boarded the 3 a.m. train to Varanasi with him. While the rest dozed off, Ummer and Shrey Avasthi stayed awake. Ummer learnt that Shrey was seventeen years old and that he lived in Delhi with his parents while his brother had moved to Australia. It was a stimulating conversation for Ummer, this narrative of a life so different from his own.

When Shrey learnt that Ummer was from Kashmir, he couldn't hide the incredulous look on his face. Ummer didn't miss it, as he was used to it. It was a common reaction from many people he had met on his recent travels. They assumed that all Kashmiri youth pick up guns for a living.

He explained to Shrey politely that his life was normal, like anyone else their age who lived in other parts of India. It was just the circumstances that were not. Shrey did not mean to hurt Ummer, but he realized that his expression probably had. He was intelligent and sensitive enough to change the topic.

Unfortunately, Ummer failed his PABT written exam. Shrey passed the test but failed his air force medicals because he had an eyesight issue. However, both made it through the army medicals. They returned home with mixed feelings, each wondering if they would meet the other at the academy. The merit list was still awaited. Shrey was certain that Ummer would make it. There was, he felt, a quiet confidence and power in the other's demeanour.

Indeed, Ummer did receive a joining letter and was asked to report to the NDA, Khadakwasla, on 30 December 2012. The news spread in the village like wildfire. A few local reporters were interested in the story, and soon local newspapers featured articles along with Ummer's picture. Fayaz's chest was bursting with pride as he interacted with the press and local well-wishers, and distributed sweets to everyone in the village on this happy occasion. Uncle Hassan, whose house Ummer had nearly burnt down, was quite emotional when he came to give his nephew his blessings.

'Our naar chor has really made it big, Fayaz bhai. I couldn't be more proud of our son. He will go on to inspire many more to do something meaningful with their lives,' said Uncle Hassan, his eyes moist and brimming with emotion.

Family and friends agreed that it was the best piece of news they'd had in a long time, and gave thanks to Allah for this blessing. Usma and Asmat watched as Ummer shone in the limelight, overcome with gratitude and joy at their brother's success. Little did they realize at this point that he would be a source of inspiration for some, and of jealousy and hatred for others.

On 29 December 2012, Ummer made his maiden plane voyage from Srinagar to Pune. And on 30 December 2012, he reported at the NDA.

Chapter 10

Meeting Ummer's uncle and his family in Anantnag was high on my agenda. Ahmed Ali, whom I had got acquainted with on my first trip from Srinagar to Behi Bagh, was scheduled to pick me up.

This time Ahmed Ali made sure to stop the car near a stream and make me meet the boy who had thrown a stone on his car and me, who was there to apologize.

'Where did you get him from, Ahmed bhai?' I asked.

'He is a local boy, ma'am. He has come to apologize.' Ahmed hit the boy's head and asked him to apologize to me.

I just smiled and asked him to study. That's what all elders do and in comparison to him, I was old enough.

'Ma'am, I didn't want you to leave Kashmir with a bad opinion about us. We treat our guests like we treat God. When you go back, say nice things about us,' Ahmed said with folded hands and it made me very emotional.

We drove ahead on a happy note.

The previous night, I had met up with Colonel C.P. Singh over dinner. I was pensive, lost in a far-from-pleasant maze of thoughts about the startling opinions of students I had met in JNV, Anantnag, the graffiti on the walls in praise of Burhan Wani, and the anti-India slogans I'd seen on the way back to the camp. I consider myself a secular Indian and popular support for militancy in some areas often defies my understanding.

'The people of Kashmir don't like us at all, do they?' I asked abruptly.

Colonel Singh was slow to react, but he smiled like he had been asked this question more than once before.

'I saw really jarring graffiti today: "Indians are dogs", "Burhan Wani is still alive in our hearts", "Indians, go away from our land". I mean . . .! What are we doing here then, sacrificing the lives of soldiers every day?'

'That is a wrong assumption in my opinion, ma'am. Not every Kashmiri feels that way. The extremists, who are religiously or politically motivated, instigate people against us. But the mere fact that we manage to comb out militants from this area on a weekly basis is due to the support of secular Kashmiris. Or else we would be sitting ducks, perfect target practice for rogue elements. And you know what they say, ma'am, nothing is ever as it seems on the outside.'

Then he called a senior JCO and said, 'Saab, please make sure all those anti-India slogans and graffiti are removed from the route that ma'am travels on. Paint over everything you see. Walls. Shutters. We don't want an Indian leaving this territory feeling that Kashmir is not a part of India. If we let that happen, then what is the point of our presence here?' The senior JCO and Colonel C.P. Singh shared a smile.

Everybody was making sure that I left Kashmir on a happy note and that was confusing me even more as to what I should be happy about.

The next day, I set out to meet Ummer's uncle and aunt. I was escorted by a jawan and Ahmed was my driver once again. Peeping out of the car windows, I realized that Colonel Singh had clearly meant business! I could see the whitewash over the graffiti on the walls and shutters, and there were men at work erasing other slogans along the route to Anantnag.

The colonel had also insisted on a jawan from Anantnag accompanying me, to help liaise with the locals. Not only did this additional security measure speak volumes of the quality of protection the army extended to outsiders in the Valley, but it was a token of these soldiers' respect for Ummer, I felt, a way of honouring his memory.

I soon reached the home of Ummer's uncle, Manzoor Ahmed Parrey and was greeted by him, his wife Fahmeeda Akhtar, and his children, Mehran and Salman. It was heartening to meet Usma, Ummer's younger sister, for the first time. It was evident she had not recovered from her brother's loss, as it was still hard for her to talk about Ummer without tearing up.

'Bhaiya would always bring me a new pen each time we met. He would tell me to study hard all the time. And it wasn't just me he would harp on. Even Mehran and Salman would hear it from him,' said Usma, pointing at her dear cousins.

'Even on his breaks from the NDA, he would spend time with Mehran and Salman, and sit down to teach them maths and science. Such selflessness in such a young boy . . .' said Fahmeeda, fresh tears flowing as she recollected those moments.

It is inevitable that people speak fondly of the deceased. No doubt, I thought, Ummer had barely lived long enough to have much opportunity to do harm. Yet, it was rare for someone so young to take on the responsibility of ensuring that his sisters and younger cousins were on the right track in their lives.

We shared some tea, many stories and a few tears that day. I could see that the family was still in shock, and that their dominant emotion was terror, a visceral reaction to losing a loved one in such a violent manner.

As I made a few notes, I suddenly wondered if Usma would accept the pen I was using, which was rather special to me, as a reminder of Ummer and his gifts to her.

'Bhaiya used to get you pens, no? I would really like you to have my lucky pink pen.'

Usma accepted this small gesture graciously. I knew it was no comparison to her beloved brother's gifts, but she surprised me with a hug. Feeling a little lighter and hoping that I had helped heal their wounds in small ways, I returned to my car to head back to 3 RR.

Noticing a BSF or CRPF jawan every few metres en route, I said to no one in particular, 'So much army presence in this area, no? Kashmir is inundated with army personnel.' The driver was suddenly all ears.

'Exactly, madam. We don't need military presence in Kashmir. If they go away, so will the militants. Their presence has caused the rise in militancy. We are generally peace-loving otherwise,' lamented Ahmed.

The jawan, a Kashmiri from the locality, also agreed with him vehemently. I wasn't expecting that at all, but in Kashmir, one had to be prepared for anything.

'If Kashmiri militants lay down their guns, the army will gladly go away,' I retorted.

Ahmed sensed from my tone that he shouldn't argue further, and changed the topic.

'Madam, there is a famous Pashmina shawl merchant in the area. Would you like to buy some for yourself or your mother maybe?'

'I'm too tired to shop today, Ahmed,' I lied. I was actually too scared to venture out to unknown places.

Ahmed wasn't one to give up easily, though.

'No problem, madam. I will have him sent to your room. He has permission from the army to do so,' he reassured me.

'Maybe after lunch tomorrow then,' I said, to buy some time to go over my notes and plan questions for the interviews scheduled for the next day.

Ahmed dropped us off at the gate and the jawan walked me to the barrier.

'Bhaiya, you also feel that the army isn't required here?' I asked.

'*Memsaab, CO saab ke liye jaan de denge par bewajah kyon marein.* I have family living outside the camp, and in the town, we agree with the locals. Always. To keep my family safe.'

Life in this turbulent region was infinitely complicated, I realized, and so I had nothing further to say.

'So, were you happier today, ma'am?' Colonel Singh inquired when I met him at dinner, referring to the whitewashed graffiti and slogans.

'Infinitely happier,' I exaggerated, to show some gratitude for the lengths that they had gone to in order to keep the image of Kashmir intact in the mind of one Indian. 'But why *do* we need the army here, Colonel? Can't this place do without military presence?'

'Ma'am, if we leave this place to them, it'll be mayhem. We've spent a lot of money building infrastructure in this state. The militants will blow it all up in a day. They don't really care for the state or its people. Their crazy ideology is all that matters to them. These gun-toters want to bring in Sharia law. They know a democratic country like India is governed by its Constitution, not religious laws. But they have zero regard for the Constitution and for law enforcement.'

He paused and continued, 'We lose more men in this area than we ever have in any other deployment. So if we weren't convinced that the civilians of Kashmir needed our protection, we would have exited a long time ago.'

'But militants also get killed and their families too,' I said, to keep him talking.

'Of course they do. But the reasons cannot be compared. We are here legitimately, to discharge our duties. We are here to protect the freedom and sovereignty of our nation. This is more real than the illusion of a few misinterpreted fundamentalists. If we leave, mark my words, these guys will die killing one another. We are only protecting them from themselves.'

I was almost sure that most of the Kashmiris wouldn't have agreed with that statement. For that matter, every individual would want to be free in order to be happy and in pursuit of that happiness, Kashmiris hate the military presence in their area.

'For every victory, we also suffer heavy losses. Just a few days ago, we were able to find and shoot Hizbul Mujahideen

(HM) Commander Yasin Yatoo. But then, we also lost two of our boys.' The colonel looked helpless for a moment.

After some more conversation with him, I retired to my room. But Ahmed hadn't forgotten his promise to bring his friend, Shaukat Ali, the Pashmina shawl-seller, to the camp. Promptly, after lunch, they were at my door with their wares and every intention of swindling me.

While he was showing me his beautiful shawls, Shaukat Ali suddenly said, 'Madam, I heard that you are writing a book on Ummer Fayaz.'

I nodded.

'Do you know who killed him?'

'Do *you* know who killed him?' I countered.

'Madam, he was involved with the daughter of the DSP of that area. And the DSP had him killed. Make sure to write that in your book.'

I struggled to keep my expression neutral. This place never ceased to surprise me. I also wondered what the DSP of Shopian, Ashiq Hussain Tak, a highly decorated police officer as well as an investigating officer in Lieutenant Ummer Fayaz's murder, would say to this theory. I was due to meet him next, in Behi Bagh, and I resolved to find out.

Just before I left for Behi Bagh, Colonel Singh called for me and said, 'Ma'am, Lieutenant General Sandhu, the corps commander of 15 Corps, is here to felicitate the officers involved in the operation.'

I managed to wrangle fifteen minutes with General Sandhu. I had just one question for him. A pertinent one for me.

As I waited outside the briefing point to meet him, I saw a group of young officers standing in a row. They were the ones who had conducted the successful operation that ended in the capture and killing of one of the most wanted terrorists in the area.

'Sir, will the killing of Lieutenant Ummer Fayaz be avenged?' I looked straight into the eyes of General Sandhu when I asked him that question.

'Of course, he was our boy and we won't let the killers get away with the murder,' was his reply, as he stared right back into mine.

My doubts were assuaged. That was all I wanted to hear. Period.

Chapter 11

The irony of it was not lost on Ummer. He had planned to conquer the skies as a pilot, and was instead making his very first journey by air to join the army. It dawned on him that while he had complete control over his own choices, it remained to be seen what destiny had in store for him.

Young Ummer entered the portals of the NDA with great nervous energy. He still remembered his first day away from home at JNV, with all his senses working overtime to adjust to the new environment. Day 1 at the NDA was similar, except that he was considerably older and had done this before. He was able to recall and tap into the wisdom of his previous experience to negotiate this new milestone.

So, here he was. Cadet Ummer Fayaz at the NDA, Pune. To begin on a fresh slate, he would have to unlearn many things, and clear away the cobwebs of his previous attitudes and assumptions. There was no other path to becoming a good officer. And stubborn though Ummer was, this was going to be no mean task. He needed all the determination and willpower he could summon to help him through the inevitably tough days ahead at the NDA.

On the first day, he was awestruck at the sheer expanse of the campus. He had only managed to see a small part of it during the initial orientation activities, but there would be time for all that. His first task was to register at the Cadets' Mess gate. Then, along with some fifty batchmates, Ummer reported to Major Chetan Pandey, the adjutant. He would never forget his first glimpse of the major, an impressive figure who assembled cadets like the Phantom. He addressed the batch, and informed them that he was in charge of discipline. Afterwards, he met each cadet individually in his room, noting down their names and listing their strengths and accomplishments. Here was one officer who knew the strengths of each individual in all eighteen squadrons!

Squadrons were not very different from houses in public schools, Ummer learnt. Some 1800 to 2100 cadets are distributed equally among the eighteen squadrons at the NDA, a system that enables them to compete against each other while improving their skills.

Each squadron has its own building with an anteroom where the cadets can watch TV, a balcony, a parking area and an office for the squadron in-charge. The buildings also have recreational facilities like table tennis and pool.

One of the principles of selection to the squadrons was as random as it was fair: if a new cadet was proficient in a field that a squadron was not doing well in, the cadet was assigned to that very squadron to boost the skills of the group as well as to hone his leadership skills. Ummer told Major Chetan that he was skilled in hockey, football and cricket. Accordingly, the major decided to assign him to the Delta Squadron.

The Delta Squadron building was close to the Cadets' Mess, and Ummer made his way there on foot after his meeting with the adjutant. The first thing he noticed was the impressive stairway that presumably led up to the dorms. To the right of the stairs was the 'motivational corner', he later found out. He put his bags down in the hall to look at the picture of a youngish officer whom he felt strangely drawn to. The writing beneath the photograph said he was Lieutenant Colonel Vishwanathan, a Kargil brave heart who had lost his life during the capture of Tololing peak. There was a notice board to the left of the picture which featured instructions for the cadets, news clippings and 'a thought for the day'.

Further down the corridor, the poem 'If' by Rudyard Kipling had been framed and hung on the wall. Ummer read it for the first time that day, not knowing that this poem was going to be his constant companion over the next three years.

The NDA training programme extended over six terms, each of five months' duration with a month's leave after each term. The sixth-termers were generally appointed with responsibilities for their respective squadrons. They were called Lords. One of them was the cadet quarter master sergeant (CQMS), responsible for store supplies and logistics. He asked the new cadets to collect their kits, which contained shoes, sports gear and other necessities. As they entered the mess for dinner in formal wear, Ummer spotted Shrey from a distance. They immediately walked towards each other and shook hands warmly.

'So, did you make it to the air force?' Ummer asked.

Cadets in all defence services are first trained at the NDA, and Ummer wasn't sure if Shrey was here to train for the air force or the army.

'No, I didn't clear the medical,' Shrey smiled.

They sat next to each other at dinner that night, and Shrey told Ummer that he had been assigned to the Golf Squadron.

On Day 2 at the NDA, the Delta Squadron was asked to report to a spot near the Sudan Block, which was the administrative building. All the sixth-termers of the Delta Squadron were present that day. The first-termers, called Dopes because they were as clueless as could be at this stage, were asked to introduce themselves to the squadron. Ummer announced that he was from Kulgam district in the south of Kashmir. And he suddenly had the attention of the entire squadron. He was getting used to it by now and chose not to take offence.

During the introduction round, the seniors scanned the new cadets, trying to identify prospective Pals. Pals were cadets with the same regional, religious, caste or other affiliations. Pals were never allotted the same room, corridor or flank in the squadron, in a perfect example of the army's endeavour to balance homogeneity and heterogeneity within its ranks.

While some, like Ummer, had to do their introductions with push-ups, others had to introduce themselves with front rolls. It was all in good humour and turned out to be a great icebreaker.

Ayush Joshi, a lanky cadet, was asked to crack a joke instead. 'I couldn't crack a joke even if I tried, sir,' pleaded Ayush.

'Why not?'

'Because I don't have a hammer, sir,' he said, delivering his punchline with great comic timing.

The entire squadron burst into loud guffaws.

The second-termers were called Mysteries because they were adept at hiding themselves from their chores and seniors. Majid, a second-termer, knew that he had found a *roza* partner in Ummer. Ummer's name was a giveaway.

Majid was from Chhattisgarh, but had studied at the Sainik School, Rewa. His parents were professors in a government college. Like Ummer, he had cleared the NDA entrance in his first attempt.

'I'm your Pal,' he told Ummer with a smile.

Ummer, who had caught on to NDA lingo by now, knew exactly what he meant and smiled back.

Just then, Rakesh Choudhry came up and introduced himself to Ummer, following it up with, 'You look quite weak. Don't you eat?'

Ummer was silent, not knowing what to make of the concern that Rakesh was showing.

'Where are you from?' Rakesh persisted.

'From Anantnag, but my home is in Kulgam,' replied Ummer.

'You say he looks weak, but do you know what you look like?' Majid interjected.

'No, sir,' said Rakesh respectfully.

'You look like Mojo Jojo, the bad guy from *The Powerpuff Girls*.'

A quick smile creased Ummer's face, and it was contagious enough to spread to Rakesh. The three then burst into laughter.

It turned out that Rakesh had studied in Sainik School, Satara. His father, a subedar in the army, had been posted to Kashmir, and he was aware of the situation in the Valley.

After the meeting, Majid walked Ummer to the room allocated to him. Entering his dorm, Ummer saw Ayush Joshi, the hammer joke guy, sitting on one of the two beds in the room. They had barely said hi when a dark-complexioned boy, who was slightly overweight by NDA standards, walked in.

'Hey guys, I'm Vishwanath Bhoi.' Then, addressing Ummer, he said, 'I heard that you are from Kashmir.'

Not sure if he was going to be hated or liked for the fact, Ummer nodded quietly.

'My father was posted in Udhampur from 1999 to 2004. Nice to meet you, man.'

'Was he in the army?' asked Ayush.

'Yes! We got a taste of the Kargil War and the people who fought in it. I also got to meet a lot of Kashmiris while dad was posted there. So I can imagine that it wasn't easy for you to join the NDA.'

'Well, not many people really know that I joined the NDA,' Ummer said in a low voice.

'I completely understand,' said Bhoi.

Distrust comes easily to Kashmiris who grow up in the Valley. But somehow, Ummer didn't feel threatened by Bhoi's claim to familiarity with his complicated background.

On Day 3 at the NDA, Majid introduced Ummer and Ayush to Amlan Acharya.

'He is your overstudy,' Majid said by way of introduction.

Seeing the confused look on their faces, he explained, 'He is the equivalent of your mother at home. While you're here at the academy, he will be your mother, responsible for you on every count.'

Amlan, a third-termer, was considered old enough to take on mentorship roles.

'When you didn't perform well in school, did your mother hit you?' he asked, and Ummer and Ayush nodded.

'If you had negative feedback during a parent-teacher meeting, would she not punish you?'

They nodded in unison.

'And if you were a fussy eater, would she yell at the top of her voice?' Affirmative, again.

'Well, I will be doing just about the same with you two.'

As the first term progressed, Ummer quickly realized that navigating the academy was akin to walking on quicksand. The more you retaliated against the nature of the sand, the more likely you were to sink. Acceptance was key.

Ummer wasn't sure if he was going to be popular at the academy like he had been in his school. He was used to being liked instantly. However, he decided that he was not going to try to win friends or please people here. He was just going to be himself, he resolved. Initially, he was acutely conscious of the fact that he belonged to a minority. But he soon perceived that his fears were unfounded. The Indian Army was probably the most secular organization he had encountered in his life.

Cadets who came with misguided expectations, of proving their valour by playing out childhood fantasies of uniforms and guns and covert operations, were soon rudely awakened to the reality and rigour of army training.

'Please follow me,' Amlan instructed Ummer and the other first-termers. It turned out he was giving them a guided tour of the NDA. At the Sudan Block, Amlan stopped to explain the legacy behind the building and its name.

'Indian soldiers made a significant contribution in Sudan during the African campaign of World War II. This block is in honour of our contributions to the war effort. The then ambassador of Sudan to India, Rahmatullah Abdulla, inaugurated this block on 30 May 1959.'

A little further were the academic blocks. The science block was called the Rakesh Sharma Block. Ummer was particularly interested in the social science block as he knew he would be taking most of his academic classes in its halls. Amlan informed them that it was named the Manoj Pandey Block.

'Do you know who Manoj Pandey was?' he asked, not really expecting an answer.

'Yes sir! He was the officer who wrote in his dossier that he wanted to be awarded the Param Vir Chakra, the highest gallantry award. And he was the Batalik war hero who *was* awarded the Param Vir Chakra, though posthumously.'

Ummer seemed to know what he was talking about, and both the cadets and Amlan were taken aback.

'So what will you write in your dossier?' Amlan asked them. That seemed to encourage some thinking, as all the cadets suddenly fell quiet.

Again, it was Ummer who spoke up first, 'I don't know sir, but I don't want to die to change things. If I die, who will change things in my state?'

A dossier was a document maintained by the divisional officer of every squadron which was updated periodically.

The first half contained a cadet's personal information and his goals. The second half recorded his performance over all six terms of training.

Amlan then took them to Gole Market which had been a favourite hangout for NDA cadets since time immemorial. Ummer was going to spend most of his Sundays there with his friends. At the market, Ummer spotted a phone booth at a juice bar and slipped off quietly to quickly use the facility to dial a number. A man answered, and he quickly hung up.

On Day 4, a corporal who was a fifth-term appointment led the first-termers to the Hut of Remembrance. The corporal explained, 'This place is more sacred than any temple for a Hindu, Gurudwara for a Sikh, or a mosque for a Muslim. This is where we will witness and honour true self-sacrifice. Even the gods are envious of the names carved here for their sheer bravery and their lives offered in sacrifice to the nation.'

The corporal's speech and the sheer energy of the place brought on goosebumps for everyone present. Ummer was reminded of the lives that had been lost in Kashmir in the name of jihad, but he couldn't help thinking that the soldiers' sacrifice was far more honourable. His faith in the army and his reasons for joining the NDA were reinforced by this visit. He was convinced now that his decision was in alignment with what he wanted to do with his life.

The following days were spent in getting accustomed to the rules and regulations at the academy. Ummer and the other cadets were given the *katora* cut, a distinct haircut that sealed their alliance with the NDA, Pune. The cadets were also issued numbered bicycles, commonly called bikes. The bikes had to move in squads of four, five or six. If fewer than the squad's usual number of bikers were available, the ones who turned up had to run alongside their bicycle instead of riding it. Ummer's bike was number D-32, and he looked at it in utter bewilderment. Of all things, he had never expected to ride a bicycle. Never having learnt to cycle as a child, he would have to find his balance first. Much like he would have to strike a balance in his life at the NDA.

The campus was spread over a vast expanse of 8000 acres. Like most new recruits, Ummer surveyed his surroundings, wondering if he would get to see it all before he was through with his course. Little did he realize that he was going to step on almost every patch of land on that enormous campus long before his first term was over.

The fifteen-day honeymoon period of induction flew by. Even before he knew it, Cadet Ummer was up at 0400 hours, reporting for muster fall-in (morning roll-call). PT and drill practice followed. Being strong and light in build helped him get through physical training. Drill was a different story: endless hours of standing at attention, marching, turns and salutes were required to pass the Drill Square Test (DST). Effectively, it trained cadets to move, dress and obey commands like soldiers.

The adjutant, also known as the academy ghost or phantom, along with his drill staff, stringently inspected the DST. The slightest slip-up in turn-out or drill and the cadets would find themselves having to reappear for the test.

Ummer couldn't get his head around the drill, and felt his body was ill-suited for it. He swung left when he was meant to swing right. And he turned right when the rest of the platoon turned left. This went on for weeks until it was quite clear that he wasn't going to pass the test in his first term.

He proved to be a champion runner, however. It was as if he was born to run. Nevertheless, running a 14-km course was not something he was prepared for. In his attempts to not fall behind, Ummer overexerted himself and ended up with a stress fracture. He reported in sick and was treated for the fracture. But recovery took its own sweet time, and it seemed as if falling behind in the course was inevitable.

'What happened?' Majid asked Ummer when he saw him limping towards the squadron building.

'I have a stress fracture, sir. I had to report in sick,' Ummer replied. Majid grimaced, clearly not pleased with the decision.

'Report sick only when absolutely necessary! If you miss out on the course for too long, you may be relegated to the next batch. And if that happens too often, you fail the course altogether.'

Ummer nodded in understanding. It all made sense. The pro-tip was to not fall ill in the first place. And if one did fall sick he was not supposed to report it. After only a few days of rest, Ummer was back to the grind.

Academic sessions began at 0830 hours, after breakfast. And cadets were meant to use their bikes to commute to their classes. Cadets were disciplined if their squad formation was not followed, and even if bikes were not dismounted in front of other squadrons or the Sudan Block as a mark of respect. The punishments ranged from running with the bikes lifted over their shoulders to doing shoulder presses with them.

Ummer found himself face to face with this contraption on the first day of classes, wondering how to ride it. Having learnt that time was not a luxury he had, he simply picked the bike up and started running towards his classroom. Unfortunately for him, he ran straight into the CQMS, who was concerned that he had been handed a faulty bike.

'No sir!' Ummer shouted in trademark cadet fashion.

'Then form a squad and ride it. Only when you are punished will you carry your bike and run,' the CQMS commanded.

He waited for the CQMS to leave and then joined his friends—Ayush, Bhoi and Rakesh.

'How does one ride this damn thing?' Ummer asked, kicking his bicycle.

'Don't do that! Remember she's going to be your companion for the next four years. Take good care of her or you will be in trouble,' said Ayush, who was the most disciplined of the lot according to some and the most scared according to others.

'But I don't know how to ride it! Of what use is it to me?' cried Ummer.

'You have to first learn to mount her. Once that is done, the rest is instinct and you just cruise along,' Bhoi explained to Ummer, but his sing-song tone told the others that he was getting a little carried away.

'O Halwai! Are you sure that you're talking about riding a bicycle?' Rakesh asked Bhoi, who got his nickname from the Hindi term for sweetmaker. His reverie rudely disrupted, Bhoi looked visibly embarrassed at the question. The other boys chuckled at his discomfort.

'Okay, come on Ummer! Let's start with how to get on this bike,' said Ayush, straddling the bicycle to start the demo.

Ummer followed suit.

'Now you have to trust that I won't let go and pedal with both legs. Okay?'

Ummer was grateful for the lesson, and after a few failed attempts, was off to a wobbly start. In less than an hour, Ayush also taught him to propel the bike forward by using one leg to kick the ground and then pedalling with both legs once the bike was off to a rolling start.

Ummer was euphoric. It wasn't going to be such a disaster after all! The boys set off for Manoj Pandey Block with Ummer now actually riding his bike. As they approached the parking space at their academic block, the rest eased to a stop while Ummer panicked and rode straight into a neatly parked row of bikes. They toppled like a house of cards. The other cadets who witnessed this scene were in splits. They all ran forward to help Ummer and to prop up the fallen bikes, their shoulders shaking with uncontrollable laughter.

Ummer couldn't help but laugh at himself too. After all, he had made progress in leaps and bounds in a single day, and was already less sensitive about his 'disability'.

After class, he was finally able to participate in squad formation. This involved a very intricate set of rules and rigorous practice.

'Sudan-Sudan', 'Social-Social' or 'Science-Science' were the calls that filled the air outside the academic block after class, soliciting cadets who would travel in the same direction. Accordingly, cadets paired up in squads of three, four or five, and rode together. The most junior cadets were on the right of the front row of the squad. And the seniors took positions on the right of the last row.

Every now and then, the squad would pass an officer or instructor, and it was the duty of the most junior cadet to yell, '*Savdhaan*'. The alerted squad would immediately dismount and stand at stiff attention. When the officer had passed, the most senior cadet would yell, '*Vishram*', for all the cadets to relax their stance.

Ummer suffered a great deal during these routines in his early days at the academy. He would often drag his bike to the blocks after either deliberately puncturing the tyre or breaking off a small part, and try to get an excuse slip from a senior. It was a quick hustle to escape punishment for falling off the bike or not dismounting on time. But this ruse had not cured his anxiety on this count because he knew that it was only a matter of time before someone hauled him up.

On the evening of the day Ummer had learnt to ride his bike, Bhoi asked how come Ummer had not tried a bicycle in his childhood.

'In the hills, we graduate straight to motorbikes when we are old enough,' Ummer said with a note of pride in his voice. He loved the place where he belonged. It made him feel special and unique in many unexplainable ways.

The next skill he had to master was swimming. Ummer had not even seen a swimming pool until he came to the academy. He watched as his seniors swam effortlessly, all limbs synchronous in fluid motion. But it turned out that he didn't need to worry. Ummer turned out to be a water baby, a complete natural in the pool. He learnt how to float on his front and back in three days. And he had his freestyle, backstroke and breaststroke looking quite decent in fifteen days.

Ayush, on the other hand, was initially getting nowhere. Now Ummer could finally return the favour for the bike lessons, and helped him get the basics right.

All the instructors were officially called 'Ustad' but addressed as 'Saab' by the cadets. Lieutenant Jagira, the ustad for swimming, had his job cut out for him. Every cadet was required to pass a 50-metre swim test, which was mandatory for course completion. In each fresh batch, there would be some first-timers, like Ummer and Ayush, and others at varying levels of proficiency. In all his years of service, Lieutenant Jagira had never been known to give up on a cadet and usually had them all swimming like fish before they knew it.

Sundays were bliss. Ummer and his friends would go to Gole Market. When the Internet facility was working, which wasn't often, he would try to get in touch with Javed, Zainub, and his love, Tahzun, through Facebook.

Zainub was now a student of political science at Jamia Millia Islamia University, Delhi. Javed, never the academic type, had stayed back in Kashmir and was still struggling to find a foothold in a suitable professional course.

As for Tahzun, one Sunday at Gole Market, the juice shop owner Rakesh walked up to Ummer, looking annoyed.

'Did you call this number?' he asked angrily, showing him a number on his mobile.

Ummer recognized the number instantly but feigned ignorance, his expression giving nothing away.

'I get a call from this number every single day. And when I pick up, no one talks,' the owner complained.

Ummer immediately felt a pang of pain. He knew it must have been Tahzun calling for him. He had avoided calling her since that first day at the market, afraid that her father would pick up again. The last thing he wanted was to get her into any sort of trouble. He asked for the owner's phone at once, walked away from the table and dialled her.

While the phone rang, Ummer's heart pounded against his chest. After an eternity, a soft voice answered, 'Hello.'

'Tahzun, it's Ummer,' he said, stating the obvious. Ummer apologized for not calling earlier and explained his predicament. They spoke at length about his course and she told him that she missed him. When he got back to the table, he was grinning from ear to ear, and looked like he had just won the lottery.

'Girlfriend?' Bhoi asked. Ayush and Rakesh looked up at their friend expectantly. The smile on Ummer's face said it all. The boys teased him mercilessly, and also accused him of keeping them hungry while he chatted on the phone.

'Twenty paranthas, six cold drinks, three tandoori chickens and three dals,' Bhoi rattled off when the waiter came to take their order. The man wasn't surprised; the appetite of the cadets was legendary in these parts. They burned more than they ate, despite the disproportionately large meals they seemed to consume. Their course would only get more physically intensive with every term, ensuring that they stayed perpetually hungry.

When the order arrived, there was uncharacteristic silence as the four boys lunged at their food immediately.

They didn't speak a word during the meal except to ask someone to pass a dish or the jug of water.

The boys had all lost weight. Except for Bhoi, who was told that he was overweight by NDA standards. No matter how strenuously he worked out every day, his weight simply would not budge on the scale. It was another one of those damning parameters: follow, or face relegation.

'Oye! Let's go. Fall in line,' Ayush suddenly announced when he noticed the time.

The five months passed in what felt like a week. Before they knew it, it was time for their first-term break.

Ummer and the other first-term cadets were about to embark on a journey like no other, on the NDA special train that runs between Pune and Delhi. This was a privilege accorded only to NDA cadets. No amount of money or influence can buy a non-cadet a ticket on that train. When they reached the station, the seniors made them do push-ups on the platform. They repeated the performance at every station the train stopped at, much to the amusement of the civilians watching.

On reaching Delhi, the first thing that Ummer did was to meet Zainub. They had months of catching up to do. Both friends had changed in physical appearance since they had last met. Ummer was now leaner and stronger; Zainub, on the other hand, had gained a little weight. They were extremely happy to see each other again.

'Now you're an army man! You're one of them!' Zainub exclaimed.

Ummer wasn't sure if his friend was pleased with the fact. Where he came from, not many were admirers of the Indian Army. But his friend seemed genuinely happy for him.

'Did you tell Asmat and Usma that you're coming home?' Zainub asked.

'Nope! I'll just land up there and surprise them,' said Ummer. Ummer's vacation plans were always erratic and full of surprises. He had no inkling yet of the surprises life was going to throw his way.

He was eager to reach home, but made it a point to visit all his relatives before he met his parents and sisters. He went first to his uncle's home in Anantnag. His cousins were taught an entire school year's worth of the science and math syllabus in one week.

'You're so intelligent, Ummer bhaijaan. When I grow up, I want to be just like you,' Salman said to his older cousin admiringly. Ummer, in his characteristic style, brushed off the compliment. He knew that his cousin had it in him to make something of himself, and told Salman so in no uncertain terms.

He also made sure to visit his school and pay his respects to his former teachers. They were all happy to see him and seemed very proud of him. He met his juniors who were especially impressed with the way Ummer looked and talked. They asked him a million questions, and were fascinated with his description of Pune and how different it was from Kashmir.

'Will you help us prepare to join the NDA, Ummer bhaiya?' many asked, and Ummer couldn't have been happier to comply.

Strangely, it is human nature to either want everyone to be like oneself, or to want to be like everyone else. Very few people are comfortable being unique. Ummer, for one, wished for more youngsters from his community to have a better life. And maybe, as a Kashmiri in the Indian Army, there was an unconscious urge to find safety in numbers.

A week after Ummer had arrived at his uncle Manzoor's home, the latter called Jameela, 'We are coming to visit you tomorrow. I hope we will all get to eat some of your delicious chicken.'

Ummer had roped his uncle into his plot to surprise the family. 'Bhaijaan, is it only you and Fahmeeda or are Mummy and Papa coming along too?' Jameela asked, referring to Ummer's paternal grandparents who were in Anantnag.

'We are all coming, bhabhijaan,' Manzoor replied.

Jameela was very pleased at the idea of the impending visit and hurried to her kitchen at once. Asmat and Usma helped plan the menu and prepare some dishes that would be cooked early the next morning. Asmat was then in Class X, and Usma in Class VII.

Around noon the next day, Asmat opened the door to find her Uncle Manzoor, Aunty Fahmeeda and her grandparents standing rather oddly in a semi-circle. In minutes, there was happy chaos, as Ummer stepped out from behind them. His family was ecstatic at the unexpectedness of it, as Ummer had been telling them all the while that he would come home only after another three months.

'Why didn't you tell us, bhaiya?' complained both his sisters.

'If I had told you, I would have missed watching this smile and excitement on your faces. This is so much more fun,' he beamed.

Happy chatter filled the air at this impromptu family reunion. When the family sat down to eat, Ummer looked eagerly for his favourite chicken dish. But his anticipation was short-lived.

'Why is the chicken so bland?' he asked, tasting it and pulling a face.

'Because this chicken was cooked for your grandfather,' said Jameela, fondly tousling her son's hair. 'Besides, you deserve some punishment for springing this surprise on us.'

The girls laughed at this, but Jameela promised him the best food that she was capable of cooking for the rest of the time that he was there, and offered him kheer in compensation. It was Ummer's favourite dessert since he was a child.

The next day, Javed arrived to meet Ummer and there was another round of happy greetings. Ummer wanted to meet Tahzun at any cost, and Javed helped him plot their meeting. The two set off for Ganderbal one day on this secret mission.

Ummer saw her from a distance at first and waved. She ran up to him and hugged him. He kissed her gently on the forehead and held her for a long time.

He noticed that she looked different, a little taller and more grown-up than he remembered her. She looked shyly at him and said, 'Stop looking at me like that.'

'Like what?' he teased.

'Like that! So intensely!'

He laughed at that and said that he couldn't help it, that it had been too long. Tahzun and Ummer then spent some time in each other's arms beside a lake, talking about nothing and everything. Javed stood guard some distance away.

'Why did you cut your hair so short?' she asked, feeling the buzz of short hair just beginning to grow out on his head.

'Ah, this is unavoidable at the NDA. It's mandatory for cadets to get a haircut every Sunday.'

'I hope you haven't told too many people at home that you are at the NDA.' She was worried for him.

'Don't you worry so much. Only my family and close friends know,' he pacified her.

'Your name was in the newspaper, Ummer. Everyone knows that you were the only boy from Kashmir who was selected for admission to the NDA. How long do you think this will remain a secret?'

Ummer was undoubtedly fooling himself, like the proverbial ostrich. 'Only if you understand and accept that there is danger, will you be able to escape it,' Tahzun continued, exasperated.

'How can I be in danger from my own people, Tahzun? Don't worry,' he said, pulling her closer into his arms.

They sat silently for a long time until Javed came to remind them that it was time for them to leave as it was getting dark.

A few days after he met Tahzun, Ummer returned to his academy, travelling via Delhi and onward to Pune. An NDA bus took the cadets from the station to the campus, and Ummer noticed two boards at the entrance, the same ones he had seen when he had come for the first time—'Welcome to NDA', and 'You're entering a wildlife sanctuary'. Ummer had to smile. After the experience of the first term, the message from the second board seemed a fitting description of life at the NDA

Chapter 12

I only had a few days left before my military clearance, which allowed me to remain in Shopian district in south Kashmir, would expire. I had already made the acquaintance of Colonel Manu, the commanding officer of the area, and was now well acquainted with the protocol for most emergencies—including knowing exactly when to get under the bed and when to climb a tree.

Now all that was left to do was wait and hope that my scheduled interview with DSP Ashiq Tak would take place. Shopian was a hotbed of unrest and it kept the DSP on his toes.

While I was staying at the Behi Bagh camp, Colonel Manu received an invitation to a sports festival organized by the local police at the Boys' Degree College. I happened to witness his polite refusal to go when reminded of it, citing work commitments. I did ask him why to which he didn't give me an answer then.

The next day at dinner, I was thrilled to meet and catch up with Dr Joseph again. I updated him on the progress of my research on Lieutenant Ummer Fayaz's story. Colonel Manu was absorbed in signing some papers, distracted only when a news flash on TV said, 'Protests in Anantnag College as students object to sports festival.' The report went on to say that the hoisting of the tricolour had angered students, and that they had set the podium, the tents and the flag ablaze. However, Altaf Khan, the SSP of Anantnag, denied that any such event had taken place. By then, I wasn't surprised at that incident as I was well-acquainted with the hatred some Kashmiris had for India and, of course, the national flag.

'So now you know why I declined the invitation?' the CO asked quizzically.

Dr Joseph made no attempt to conceal his contempt for the whole affair, 'This problem will not end. No real victory is achieved even by victors of a war. There is only the stench of death. This war is in the minds of the people. One has to change their minds.'

Colonel Manu rolled his eyes. 'Dr Joseph is the only one that I haven't been able to convince in all these years. And now he is leaving the army too.'

Dr Joseph had been away from his family for four long years, and it had been an even longer eight years for Colonel Manu. Dr Joseph had finally given up and decided to leave the army to be with his family. The colonel, on the other hand, had missed the crucial years of watching his daughter grow up, and would continue to make that sacrifice.

I couldn't resist asking them why the students would not let them hoist the Indian tricolour, their own country's flag!

'This state is privileged to have its own flag, as you probably know. And some only want that flag to fly high,' explained Colonel Manu.

I had heard about the Kashmiri flag and knew it had history and significance.

'But couldn't both be hoisted in harmony? After all, this is their country too,' I protested.

'Ma'am, did you know that Dr Joseph is leaving us because he is being tried for treason?'

Dr Joseph looked as bewildered as I was.

'Now if I repeat that story a few times, complete with doctored videos and audio of Dr Joseph committing treason,' the CO continued, 'you will eventually believe that Dr Joseph is the bad guy.'

'I would also use my discretion, in this day and age of fake media and false propaganda. I would be careful not to get carried away,' I countered.

'Now imagine that the same news came to you from your own family. Your parents and grandparents, your aunts and uncles. Would you still be using your discretion or would you be inclined to trust their side of the story blindly, and become quite emotional about these so-called facts?'

I had no comeback to that. I realized it was this, precisely, that was playing out with children in Kashmir.

'On the Internet these days, it is possible to spread hatred and evoke anger at the speed of light. Blogs, videos and pictures which depict men in Indian Army uniforms committing violent crimes against civilians are circulated in large numbers on social media. And I can assure you that 99 per cent of these videos are doctored. Here, look,' the Colonel said, showing me his phone.

Some of the content he showed me was indeed blood-curdling. I could imagine what it must be like to receive videos like these on WhatsApp groups, and the kind of anger they could provoke against the army.

'Who makes these videos? It's easy to tell they are fake!' I cried. I could clearly see that the combat uniform worn by the supposed soldiers in the video did not belong to the Indian Army.

'Who do you think would benefit the most from a full-blown war in India?' Colonel Manu questioned.

For me, the answer didn't need to be spelt out. Several countries, including Russia, China and the US, have called out Pakistan on harbouring terrorists. And an ex-prime minister of Pakistan, Nawaz Sharif, had as good as admitted that Pakistan played a role in allowing the terrorists who attacked Mumbai in 2008 to cross the border. Those terrorists had murdered 166 people.

'But why do the Kashmiris place their trust in Pakistani extremists?'

'Ideology, madam. It is easy to sell warped ideology in the guise of religion, and make them believe that a higher power wants them to go to war. And now we also have a new menace to deal with. There is widespread drug abuse among the youth in Kashmir today. Mind-altering drugs combined with false religious ideology is a heady cocktail mix that spells disaster. Come with me,' Colonel Manu broke off abruptly.

We followed him to a room filled with trophies and souvenirs. 'Ma'am, have you heard of Captain Pawan Kumar?'

I nodded. He was the 10 Para commando whose last FB post read, '*Kisi ko reservation chahiye toh kisiko azadi bhai, humein kuch nahin chahiye bhai bas apni razai* (Some want reservations, some even freedom, but I want nothing, just my blanket).' I knew the details because I had followed the news of his death on social media and had written a mandatory post on FB in his honour.

'It was one of our boys' birthdays and Pawan was with us here on that day. He had poured himself a drink,' he said, pointing to a glass of whisky on the shelf. 'At the time, his hand was injured. It had happened in a successful operation conducted by the team he led.'

'He had conducted two successful operations, sir. He was injured in the second one,' Dr Joseph reminded the CO.

'Yes! And he was killed in the third. Very few officers even get the chance to conduct an operation, and he had three successful ones. In the end, all that he lost was his life,' said Colonel Manu.

I knew what must have been going through his mind. The army perceives that journalists and writers are likely to be more compassionate towards the other side, as it is often taken for granted that an army man's life is meant to be sacrificed. But I simply wanted to remain neutral, as that was the only way to get to the truth of Lieutenant Ummer Fayaz's death.

The colonel continued in a soft tone, 'Just minutes after he had poured that drink, came the call about the two assholes holed up in the government-run Entrepreneurship Development Institute building. He volunteered to go, and said he would be back to finish his drink with me. I'm still waiting. This is unfinished business that will have to wait until another lifetime,' he said, pointing to the glass of whisky on the shelf.

That conversation left me heavy-hearted. The more I dwelt on the bleak and turbulent reality of Kashmir, the more disillusioned I got.

The next day, I was informed that DSP Ashiq Tak was busy and would only be able to see me the day after. An entire day wasted! I was also beginning to fear that he would not see me after all. The investigation was still in progress, and besides, the police didn't come under the purview of the army. So, in that case, there were no 'higher-ups' that I could petition for permission.

Meanwhile, Colonel Manu requested if I would spend half a day counselling students at the Goodwill School that had been renamed after Lieutenant Ummer Fayaz. I said I would, of course.

But I first needed to call the former commissioner of police, Neeraj Kumar. An officer with a distinguished service record, he was also a family friend. I had the privilege of interacting with him at length recently, as we were both on the same discussion panel at the Pune Literary Fest. I explained the situation to him and told him that it was imperative to the narrative of my forthcoming book that I interview the DSP as well as gain access to the post-mortem report, the FIR and some file pictures.

'I can't promise anything, but I will try,' he said.

Within ten minutes, I received a call from DSP Ashiq Tak himself, confirming that he would indeed see me at noon the same day. At ease now, I went ahead with the volunteer class, after a brief discussion with the faculty to get a pulse of things at the school. In the course of my interactive sessions with the Class IX and Class X students, I encouraged them to express themselves without fear of judgement or reproach. Shy and reticent at first, it took them about half an hour to open up. Then they all started talking at once. Perhaps it helped that I was a stranger and a guest lecturer.

While speaking to the children about their career goals and guiding them on how to go about achieving them, it turned out that most of them aspired to be civil servants.

'Then you should be able to formulate essays on current topics, and have a realistic and balanced approach towards handling tough situations,' I advised.

'Current topics like?'

'What have you been hearing on the news recently?'

'Triple talaq, ma'am,' some chimed.

I hesitated, realizing I was caught between a rock and a hard place with this one. Then, recalling that this generation was the future of Kashmir as well as India, I decided to go ahead with a no-holds-barred approach.

'Did the government do the right thing by banning triple talaq?' I asked.

All the girls were unanimously in favour of the government mandate, while the boys opposed it.

One boy in particular seemed more agitated than the others.

'Ma'am, triple talaq is sanctioned by the tenets of Islam and he who goes against the Quran is a kafir. So we do not need to follow the ban.'

The entire class clapped heartily at this pronouncement, including the girls who had supported the ban only minutes earlier. I decided to butt in head on, and addressed the boy directly.

'So you are saying that you would divorce your wife?' I asked.

I knew this was a tricky question as marriage was probably not even on his radar as yet. He looked flummoxed but nodded his assent.

'Girls, be careful of this one. He may be a potential divorce seeker,' I said to lighten the mood, before moving on to other topics on my agenda.

But I made sure to speak to the boy one-on-one after the session. He seemed more at ease now, so I asked him who the one person was that he loved the most in the world.

'My mother,' he said, without hesitation.

'Now imagine that your father is able to just leave her and your family one fine day by invoking the triple talaq. Would that be okay with you?'

I knew from his expression that I had got through to him. He shook his head in the negative.

'The Holy Quran lists the situations in which the triple talaq can be invoked. It also says that whenever there is a talaq, heaven weeps and the earth bursts. I'm sure your mother is a good wife and your father has no reason to leave her.'

'Yes, she is a good mother also.'

We had a long chat, and he slowly opened up to tell me about his family. His father beat his mother sometimes. That explained the aggressive element in his personality, I thought. He then confessed something that sent shivers down my spine.

'Ma'am, I was given a grenade by my bhaiya and asked to burst it when the army officers came to rename our school.'

Grave dangers to the army lurked everywhere, I was beginning to discover, even in innocent places like school buildings.

I managed to convince the boy of the futility of an action like the one he had referred to. At least for the time being.

When I got back to camp, Colonel Manu and DSP Ashiq Tak were waiting for me. My face must have been drained of blood when I walked in because the CO remarked that I looked a little pale and asked if I was all right.

'Do you know that a young schoolboy was given a hand grenade to throw at those who came for the school's renaming ceremony?' I said, my voice sounding shrill.

DSP Tak and Colonel Manu exchanged looks and smiled. Of course, they knew about it and had everything under control! I was shocked and surprised but relieved.

The DSP and I immediately got started with the interview.

'Ma'am, we've grown up listening to the stories of the bravery of Neeraj Kumar. I couldn't have declined his request. In any other circumstances, I would have avoided interviews. It's a very sensitive case, given the events. I am sure you understand.'

I had already suspected as much and thanked him for seeing me in spite of his schedule. Then I probed him on every aspect of the case, every conceivable detail of it. Finally, I asked him if I could see the case file.

'I've been sitting with you for six hours now and I'm astounded by your involvement, passion and concern. I'll show you the file.'

I realized too late that I was anything but prepared to read that post-mortem report. The pictures as well as the descriptions of his injuries were graphic. I could only imagine the horror and pain of the family on seeing Ummer's body in that state. I needed a few minutes to compose myself while going through the report and excused myself for a fair while. The DSP was very considerate.

No one deserved to die like this. God had been unfair.

Chapter 13

The new term had begun and cross-country practice was on in full swing at the NDA. The stress fracture had really begun to bother Ummer, but he remembered Majid's advice and refrained from resting or reporting in sick. He continued to run.

That year, the holy month of Ramzan was due to start in the searing heat of July. During a cross-country run with his squadron, Ummer spotted Majid running ahead of him and ran faster to catch up.

'Sir, roza starts tomorrow. Kashmir has seen the moon.'

'Yes bhai! I confirmed with my Ammi too and fasting does start tomorrow.'

Majid smiled at Ummer, not wanting to damage his morale. But he knew that only sheer grit would see them through fasting and training at the same time. And with the stress fracture, he was worried for Ummer.

They reached the end of their cross-country course, and Majid came over as Ummer was cooling down with his squadron in the parade ground.

'All set for tomorrow?' Majid inquired.

'Yes sir! It will not be the same as fasting and praying with the family back home. But I don't intend to miss roza at any cost.'

'Ummer, you will be amazed to see how well-supported we are here during the holy month. People talk of secularism in India, but the NDA truly practises it. Every Muslim cadet gets to observe his roza.'

People would never have believed this of the army back home in Kashmir. Ummer's heart felt lighter by the knowledge.

That evening, Ummer, Bhoi and Ayush were hanging out in their dorm. Cadet Madhurya Malik from Ummer's foreign language class had dropped in for a chat. Ummer introduced Malik to the boys, and Bhoi interrogated him until he was satisfied. Malik revealed that he was from Lucknow, that he was born in Shamli but had studied in Rudrapur in Uttarakhand, and that his father worked in a horticulture firm.

At this point, Majid walked in. All of them sprang to attention.

He had come to ask Ummer to wake him up the next day. He trusted his Pal in this regard more than he did his alarm clock with its seductive snooze button.

'Yes sir!' cried Ummer, to confirm that he had noted the order.

'And you, joker!' Majid was addressing Malik now.

'Yes sir,' Malik shouted.

'Run faster. You're as slow as a snail.'

'Yes sir!' Malik shouted again.

'And you, Halwai, you need to lose some weight. That Prabhu and you are both overweight, and you slow down the entire squadron!' Majid said to Bhoi.

Prabhu was another cadet from the same squadron, and it so happened that he and Bhoi bore an uncanny resemblance to each other apart from the extra pounds.

The boys relaxed when Majid left the room.

'Run fast, huh! We'll see how fast he runs from tomorrow, once he starts fasting.'

Malik was clearly not happy about being compared to a snail.

'It's all just practice, Malik. Bhoi here is a good example. He was no runner to begin with, but now he maintains good speed,' said Ummer, wanting to defuse the tension.

Still annoyed, Malik continued to defend himself, 'The legendary Vikram Batra was never a good runner, but he captured two peaks during the Kargil War. Bullets travel faster than a man, and I'm good at firing.'

'That's assuming that you have a gun to fire a bullet from. That's not always the case in a war zone. Sometimes all you have to do is run to save yourself,' Ummer said, in his old manner of calling a spade a spade.

This took Malik by surprise, and he looked a little wounded.

'Which side of the bed did you get up from this morning?' he asked Ummer, evidently wanting to divert the conversation from his own weaknesses.

'I don't know about today, but tomorrow, I'd better get up on the early side so I get some time with Allah before I begin my roza.'

'Oh, you will probably get some food before roza starts. Could I also come with you to the mess tomorrow?' Malik begged.

how to mount and dismount from their steeds. The final
session was on grooming the animals.

Concurrently, the final day of the cross-country
competition was approaching. The list of runners was to
go out on Thursday that very week, and the event itself was
on Sunday.

On Wednesday, all the cadets were exhausted from a
strenuous session of drill practice. Naturally, Ummer and
Majid were affected the most. They were still deliberating
on whether to run the 12-km cross-country course on
Sunday. Although Muslim cadets are largely excused from
physicals during roza, most of them try their best not to
miss these. However, the exhaustion they felt on this day
influenced Ummer and Majid to decide against running.

When the list of cross-country runners was presented
to Squadron Commander Lieutenant Colonel Inderjeet
Singh, he scanned the list and frowned. The colonel
was responsible for every aspect of the Delta Squadron's
performance at the NDA and nothing escaped his keen
eyes. He summoned Ummer and Majid.

'Why aren't you two running?'

'Sir, we are observing roza and are not in a position to
run,' Majid replied for the both of them.

Colonel Inderjeet looked first at Ummer and then at
Majid. 'And where in the Holy Quran does it say that you
must abandon your duties while observing roza?'

Ummer and Majid exchanged quick glances.

'Will you perform your duty or not?' Colonel
Inderjeet asked.

'Yes sir!' was the obvious reply.

But in this case, while the tongue replied in the
affirmative, heart, body and mind protested vehemently.

'Of course, you are welcome to join us but w
at around 0400 hours,' Ummer warned.

Bhoi and Ayush would also have loved
goodies, but sleep was equally dear to them. Th
unearthly hour to wake up, even for precious foo

Ummer was at Majid's room at 0300 hours s
they had their *sehri* at the mess. Roza is observed
sunrise and sunset, and those observing the fas
eat or drink anything during those hours, not eve
Surprisingly, Malik made it in time for the sehri, a
them with his enthusiasm for the special food.

The NDA mess staff did not disappoint. Th
cooked an elaborate meal for all the Muslim cadets.
evident that they had been hard at work in the ki
from midnight. The mess workers also went aroun
tables, making sure the cadets were eating well and co
them to take just a little more. Their health and well-l
was of supreme importance to the staff of the NDA. T
cadets were training to defend the nation and the acad
would do everything in its power to help them succeed

It was also the day that Ummer began learning a r
skill to add to his repertoire—horse-riding. The horses
the NDA are majestic animals. Ummer looked at them wi
awe, marvelling at their muscular structure and wonderii
how many times he was going to fall off them before h
mastered the art. After all, unlike bicycles, horses were fles
and blood and had a will of their own.

The ustads taught them a lot on the first day itself.
They started with instructions on saddling the horse, fixing
the bit and adjusting the stirrups. Then there was a brief on

On Sunday, Colonel Inderjeet was extremely pleased to see both the boys at the start line. He wished both of them the best of luck.

In truth, the determination to be a true Muslim, strengthened by the colonel's sharp reprimand, prompted them at every step of those twelve kilometres. Although they were soon dripping wet from the exertion and exhausted beyond measure, the cheers of the officers' wives and other staff at every post inspired them to keep on. At one post, Colonel Inderjeet's wife, Rajni Singh, cheered them both on by calling out their names as loudly as she could. The officers' wives often formed a special bond with the cadets and watched out for them at every step of their course.

'Ummer and Majid! Make your squadron proud!' Rajni cheered.

Ummer and Majid ran faster. At the finish line, they were so dehydrated and depleted of vital salts that their muscles were cramping. Somehow, their minds hardly registered these physical symptoms, so euphoric were they from the triumph of having run the race. Ummer and Majid had, in fact, finished in second place out of six enclosures and their run had contributed eighteen points to the squadron.

Colonel Inderjeet had served in Kashmir in the RR unit, and knew the place and its people only too well. He had seen much conflict during his posting in the state, and lost men to skirmishes with militants. In motivating the two young recruits to perform their duty despite personal limitations, Colonel Inderjeet had demonstrated how the NDA transforms cadets into officers, capable of leading men through dangerous tasks and defending the entire nation.

'True achievement is when you achieve success despite all adversities. It is hard enough for a boy from south Kashmir to make progress in any field, let alone make it to the NDA,' the colonel addressed Ummer. Having served in that area, he knew only too well what it meant for a Kashmiri boy to be an officer. 'You have done your state and your religion proud. Well done, boy!'

Ummer and Majid were in their squadron building after the race, talking about eating a whole roasted chicken and copious amounts of food after breaking their fast in the evening. The conversation in the hall died down when the cadets realized their commander was in their midst. Colonel Inderjeet praised all the athletes who had run that day, but he was particularly generous in his praise of Ummer and Majid.

'They kept spectacular timing despite the fact that they are both observing roza.'

They got a standing ovation from the crowd that day. And Malik stood there with his head bowed.

It was business as usual the next day, but the emphasis was now on academics as exams were fast approaching too. Yet, even in the midst of exam prep, PT and drill routines were not compromised.

Colonel Inderjeet kept a close watch on the cadets and their behaviour. Foreign cadets from Afghanistan, Bhutan, Bangladesh and Nepal were also enrolled at the NDA. In the interest of national security, NDA instructors are always on their guard.

Ummer's equestrian lessons were going well. His first horse looked more like a pony. Ummer deliberately chose the animal because it wasn't very tall or formidable-looking. He could mount the horse quite easily, and hoped this meant he could control it with relative ease.

'Kick the horse like I showed you,' the ustad commanded.

Ummer lightly dug his heel into the horse's flank.

'Kick harder,' the ustad shouted again.

Ummer kicked a little harder, but the horse refused to budge.

'Why isn't your horse moving?' the ustad asked.

'The horse is hungry, ustad. He says he will not move until he is fed,' Ummer joked.

'How do you know that the horse is hungry?'

'He told me in my ear, ustad. He is very shy and doesn't perform well under pressure.'

Ummer was, of course, using the horse as a metaphor. He had been observing roza for fifteen days now, and was already looking forward to Eid.

'You better kick the horse, or I will soon be kicking you and the horse.'

'No saab!' Ummer cried, managing to kick the horse hard enough to get it moving.

He began to acquire the skill, slowly, and in a few days was able to ride the horse, though not very adeptly.

'Remember, if you can control your horse, you can control almost anything,' the ustad often said.

The next milestone was the Greenhorn Camp, a four-day intensive programme that introduced second-termers to essential battle subjects such as map reading, tent pitching, fitting of web equipment, navigation, endurance training and compass reading.

After pitching their tents, they were ordered to dig trenches around it. Ummer and Rakesh happened to be working in the front of the tent while Bhoi and Ayush were digging at the back. When Rakesh returned from doing a little work on the sides of the tent, he saw Ummer sprawled on his back, resting. The rest of them were halfway through the task while Ummer had barely started. Rakesh was livid and threw a fit.

'What's wrong with you? Why aren't you digging? If we lose, it'll be because of you!' Rakesh exclaimed.

Ummer didn't take to this very kindly. He seized his pickaxe and started to dig like his life depended on it. When Colonel Inderjeet came around to inspect, he was surprised at the depth of the trench. He then lowered himself into the trench, and it was so deep that he could barely be seen from the outside. This flummoxed Colonel Inderjeet, and he double-checked with the other cadets whether only one person had dug the trench on this side. In the end, he gave their team negative marks for failing to meeting the required standards of uniform trench depth. Subsequently, the boys had a go at Ummer for overperforming and ruining it all. After Colonel Inderjeet left, all the boys ran after Ummer who sped from there as a reaction to the boys having a go at him. They all pounced on him after throwing him to the ground and punched him from all angles till he cried out an apology.

'I'm telling you that this guy has also attended the jihadi camp across the border. He has trained with the jihadis also and now he is training with us. All that training has made him superhuman.' Bhoi joked and all the others laughed, including Ummer. After the Greenhorn Camp, Ummer had a new nickname—Jihadi.

Swimming lessons continued, with Ayush still struggling. But no one in NDA gives up; rather, no one is allowed to give up. So by the end of the term, Ayush was a swimmer. Swimming was only one part of the challenge, though. The bigger challenge was the ten-metre jump. Cadets had to jump into the pool from that height. If someone jumped and landed with legs apart, their balls would literally be in their mouth. There was a very precise technique to the jump, besides conquering one's fear of heights.

Prabhu, Bhoi's doppelganger, was back at the academy after almost a month of sick leave. He had lost an astonishing amount of weight.

'What happened to you, dude? How did you become half your size?' Bhoi asked jealously.

'Dysentery, dude. Bad case of dysentery. I thought I was going to die!'

'What did you eat to get dysentery?' Bhoi was eager to know not because he was concerned about Prabhu but he also wanted to lose weight like him. Ironically, Prabhu was not privy to the secret of his own weight loss.

The second term also stepped up the pressure on the cadets to keep abreast of their academics, and five months passed in a frenzy of learning. Ummer was looking forward to going home again at the end of it all. Only this time, Javed was very concerned about his friend's safety. When Ummer reached Kashmir, the first person he met was Javed. He was there to pick him up.

'The situation here has worsened, Ummer. And that haircut of yours is a dead giveaway. Don't you know the people here hate faujis? They must already know that you are training with the NDA.'

Javed's anxiety was based on more than friendly concern. Inquiries had been made about Ummer in Kulgam, and this meant that his life could be in danger.

'Javed, I haven't harmed anyone. Why will they want to harm me?' Ummer reasoned.

'You training for the army is reason enough for them to kill you. Don't you know what the army does to us?'

The situation in south Kashmir was deteriorating by the day. More and more youth were joining militant groups. Given these circumstances, Ummer's joining the NDA stood out in stark contrast.

It was Javed who decided that Ummer's family should tell anyone who wanted to know his whereabouts that he was training to be a doctor in Pune. Ummer, on the other hand, was convinced by now that the NDA was the gateway to a noble calling, and he wanted to encourage as many of his juniors as possible to apply. Whenever he visited his former school during vacations, the juniors would badger him for all the information they could get. And Ummer was invariably generous and supportive, and had words of advice and encouragement for all.

Ummer also continued to guide his sisters in their education. Asmat was now in Srinagar, studying in senior secondary school, and Usma was all set to go to Anantnag. They were both at home in Kulgam since Ummer was on his vacation but Usma had to go out to school the next day for a practical exam. Ummer immediately offered to accompany her.

'No, bhaiya! You will not leave the house. Tomorrow is Friday, and you seem to have no clue how dangerous the situation is! I will not put my brother out there like that. You're so precious to us, bhai,' Usma said emotionally.

Ummer wasn't very keen on staying at home, though. So he decided to watch a cricket match of the Kashmir Premier League. The Indian Army under the leadership of General Hasnain had initiated the league to engage the youth in meaningful activities. For a time, it had worked and more boys had bats in their hands than guns. Ummer was happy to know what Hasnain was doing for the young boys in the Valley.

Engrossed in the game, he was taken aback when some members of the stadium staff walked briskly up to him and asked for his ID. Fortunately for Ummer, he happened to be carrying a civilian identity card.

While at home during this vacation, his haircut attracted more attention from the locals than he would have liked. But he consistently maintained that he was studying medicine. At the same time, in spite of the risks involved, Ummer more than willingly helped train juniors who aspired to join the NDA. Javed was not pleased at all with this decision, but Ummer insisted that it was a necessary risk. He just had to help as many kids from his town as possible.

A month later, Ummer was back at the academy for his third term. Cross-country practice continued, and the pain and trouble from his stress fracture persisted. To add to his troubles, new tensions cropped up in his core team and the squadron at large, on occasions when one of them fell behind or broke the rules.

Halfway through the term, a senior found pen drives in Prabhu's bag. Pen drives were a strictly prohibited item at the NDA as they could be used to leak military data. All the third-termers were summoned and the seniors watched as they did front rolls in the battalion area, followed by push-ups and then handstands. Ummer's patience ran out with the handstands. He refused, knowing what it could do to his already troubling stress fracture.

'You fool! You bloody well just do them or we will all get rogered beyond recognition,' Bhoi hissed.

'But I haven't done anything wrong to get punished like this!' cried an adamant Ummer. 'And don't you guys get it? What would happen if my leg is permanently injured? I'm the only one who made it out of there so my family pinned a lot of hope on me. And what of inspiring more Kashmiri kids to make something of themselves? I refuse to get relegated or break my leg. These seniors don't understand how important it is that I become an officer, in the larger scheme of things. If I do, more kids will likely follow suit. Perception will slowly change. We will be the bridge to a better life for Kashmiris!'

Bhoi, Malik and Ayush were upside down, their bodies propped up on their hands, while Ummer sat cross-legged on the floor, ranting. That was probably the first time his friends realized why Ummer was here, and that his ambition of becoming an army officer was driven by larger aims and loftier motives than theirs.

Soon enough, however, the seniors caught him squatting on the floor.

Predictably, they saw red.

'Why are you not in a handstand?' One of them yelled angrily.

'Sir, the pen drive was found in Prabhu's bag. Why am I being punished for it?' Ummer said, not without a hint of cheek in his tone.

'Because the pen drive was found in Bhoi's bag,' a senior replied.

'Sir, it wasn't me. It was Prabhu,' Bhoi cried out, still in handstand position.

The seniors now looked confused and went to the anteroom to do some fact-checking as Bhoi couldn't be mistaken for Prabhu any more because Prabhu had lost a lot of weight. The boys heaved a sigh of relief and lowered themselves on to the floor.

Majid arrived on the scene as soon as he heard, and tried to pacify the boys.

'Ummer, don't argue with your seniors like that! Others will also have to face the brunt of it,' he advised.

Sure enough, the very next morning, Ayush had to run with a backpack on account of Ummer's insolence the previous day. This time, Ummer truly felt sorry that someone else on his squad was suffering the consequences of his actions.

Another day, when Ummer, Ayush, Rakesh and Malik were returning from a class, while the others dismounted in front of another squadron as per the rules, Ummer didn't do it quickly enough. He went straight ahead, and when he looked over his shoulder to see if there was room for damage control, he fell. Not only did this make his leg worse, the others were also punished as a result of his slip-up. The incident bothered him so much that he began getting excuse slips thereafter to avoid riding his bike.

Taking note of this, Majid told Ummer to form a squad with him after asking the other seniors not to give him excuse slips.

'Sir, that's not a very good idea. Chances are that I will let you down.'

'But is that reason enough to abandon you?'

Ummer was taken aback by the question.

'It's like this, Ummer. Our training here is a mirror for scenes on the battlefield. If a soldier from our unit is injured and we are on the retreat, would we leave him behind? The entire team owns the consequences of the actions of its members. The good *and* the bad. And frankly, I'd rather take my chances with your wounded leg for squad formation in the NDA than haul your sorry ass on the battlefield. So humour me and get on that bike and ride, please.'

Ummer was humbled; it was a deep lesson indeed. He understood now why he was punished when he wasn't the one smuggling pen drives and why his team-mates were penalized when he couldn't maintain the squad formation. A lot changed in him after that. Profoundly. He had understood what it meant to work as a team for a much greater cause. Even if he had started out at the NDA with only a stable career in view, he had since been transformed inside out. The past year and a half of training had not only changed every cell in his body but had also strengthened his mind and core values immeasurably.

Cross-country competition was just around the corner and Ummer's stress fracture was worse than ever because of the fall from his bike.

'Oye Jihadi! Will you run the cross-country?' Bhoi asked Ummer.

'I guess not. The pain in my ankle is bad.'

'But we need you. You're one of the best runners we have. After me, of course,' Bhoi quipped.

After the talk with Majid, he wasn't about to let his buddies down. So he did run and garnered a few points for this team. But this feat took a huge toll on his injured leg. Ummer was admitted to the hospital as the pain was now almost unbearable. He was discharged a week later.

At the end of the third term, Ummer realized he couldn't go home. He received a call from Javed, warning him not to come home as some people had been inquiring about him in the village. This time, they had asked Javed directly.

Ummer wondered how he was going to explain his decision to stay back to his trainers at the academy. He didn't want to reveal the situation at home to them for fear that they might even suspect him of precisely the kind of activities that would endanger his life in Kulgam.

Ummer decided to approach his squadron commander despite his misgivings. He often felt that Colonel Inderjeet observed him closely and suspected him because he was a Kashmiri. The colonel kept an eye on everyone in his squadron primarily because it was his duty to do so. At the same time, he was aware that, with his Kashmiri background, Ummer was exceptionally vulnerable. Militants recruited boys like Ummer by the dozen. Making sure that he was integrated into the NDA community while ensuring that he was unaware of the effort this took, was quite the challenge for his squadron commander.

Ummer told Colonel Inderjeet that he didn't want to risk travelling with his bad leg, and wanted to use the vacation to rest his injured limb on campus. The colonel thought nothing of it, and informed Ummer that he would be staying with him and his family. The mess wasn't open to cadets during term break, he said, and they would enjoy having Ummer over during the vacation.

The Colonel's wife, Rajni, took good care of Ummer during the week that he spent with them. She asked after his family and the situation back home, but Ummer wasn't very forthcoming for fear of being judged.

A week later, Ummer went to see his friend Zainub in Delhi. He had called home once again before making these plans, just in case the situation had improved and there was a slim chance that he could go see his family. His father sounded very sure, however, that he did not want Ummer to come to Kulgam. His Aunt Fahmeeda insisted that he stay with her brother Rahmat and his wife in Delhi. Not wanting to distress them any further, he went to see his Uncle Rahmat who was very happy to receive him.

Chapter 14

Now that I had interviewed DSP Ashiq, it was time to head back. A new cab driver, Shabeer, was scheduled to drop me to Srinagar airport. His name rang a bell, but I couldn't remember why.

A jawan accompanied me from Behi Bagh this time. Every time the army took special measures for my safe travel, I worried that it meant there would be fresh dangers lurking en route or that the general situation in the Valley had deteriorated.

I could tell that Shabeer wanted to start a conversation with me but he seemed very conscious of the jawan's presence in the car. Eventually he couldn't contain himself and asked, 'Madam, you are writing a book on Ummer Fayaz?'

How the hell did he know?

'Madam, it was I who found the officer's body.'

Of course! This was Shabeer, the cab driver who had first spotted Ummer in the early hours of that fateful day at the chowk. I sat up straight, my mind on high alert.

'Really? Tell me everything you know from the beginning,' I said. Shabeer proceeded to tell me how he happened to find Ummer's body.

To his credit, he didn't stray far from the facts documented in the confidential police investigation report.

'I didn't even know whose body it was, madam. There was blood everywhere, and I could see that it had been a violent death. So I had no choice but to run. Reporting a criminal act would put me at risk as I would be the first suspect. I have mouths to feed,' said Shabeer, in a desperate effort to absolve himself of guilt for running from the crime scene.

'Did you know Ummer?' I asked.

'Yes madam, I knew him. And I know his family very well. I also know the suspects, and they weren't the ones who killed Ummer. In fact, the suspects met Ummer's father and told him that they were innocent. The murder hasn't gone down well with the locals. He was a young boy who had done no harm to anyone. He didn't deserve to die. And definitely not in the way that he did.'

'Are you saying that you support the terrorists, Shabeer bhaiya?'

'No madam, I don't support either side. Not the army and not the terrorists. There was a time when I felt a little more sympathetic towards the terrorists. But one fine day, when I personally bore the brunt of their activities, I stopped supporting them.'

'Really? What happened *one fine day*?' I said sarcastically, unable to disguise my anger.

'Madam, we were expecting a baby and my wife's water broke. As we were rushing her to the hospital, some protests took place. I pleaded with the protestors to let us through as I was a civilian and known to most of them. But they were mad with rage from the poison fed to them by the propagandists. They didn't let us through and we lost our baby that day.' Shabeer was teary-eyed. 'So from that day on, I don't side with anyone. I only work and get back home and pray for peace. And pray that no one loses a child like we did.'

At the airport, I called DSP Ashiq to tell him what Shabeer had told me—that the suspects had visited Ummer's father to tell him that they were innocent. I was worried for Ummer's family. They had already been through the horrific nightmare of losing their only son. I hoped this visit wasn't a veiled threat, some tactic to subtly coerce Fayaz into cooperating with them or to warn him of dire consequences should they be harmed by the army or the police.

DSP Ashiq didn't seem surprised.

'The innocent don't need to give an explanation,' he said simply.

I asked him then if he was better and healing fast. He brushed the question off nonchalantly.

'I'm fine, ma'am. This is the state of affairs now. We are just happy to get home each day and see the next dawn break.'

I had heard that DSP Ashiq needed nine stitches on his forehead after a notorious stone-pelter had managed to wound him in Memender. He had caught this particular miscreant, but just before that, he had been attacked by a mob and a stone had hit him in the chest as well.

After speaking to DSP Ashiq, I realized I had a half-hour left till boarding time. The Gulshan bookstore was close to my terminal and I decided to visit it again. The shopkeeper recognized me and started a conversation.

'I'm an author, and I'm writing a book on Lieutenant Ummer Fayaz. Have you heard of him?' I asked.

'Yes, I've heard of him. But you know, madam, there was an innocent shepherd boy who was killed by the forces yesterday. He was mistaken for a terrorist. I'm pretty sure no one will write a book on him,' he said, obviously unsympathetic to my cause.

I had barely landed in Bengaluru when I heard the news of the killing of a twenty-three-year-old jawan, Irfan Ahmad Dar, who had gone missing on Friday, 24 November 2017. His bullet-riddled body was found in Shopian district the next morning. The cowardly attack bore an eerie resemblance to the death of BSF jawan Ramzan Parray, who was also shot dead by terrorists while on vacation at his residence in September 2017.

The police had launched an investigation into the murder, and the hunt for the gunmen was on. It seemed as if getting away with Ummer's murder had emboldened the terrorists and they were on a killing spree, targeting the army and the police, trying to replicate their first success.

The wait was agonizing, for the family and for me. I often called DSP Ashiq for news of progress on the case. I don't think anybody except the family wanted a closure on this more than me.

Meanwhile, my research on Ummer Fayaz led me to a whirlwind of interviews. Straight after DSP Ashiq Tak, I was scheduled to meet Ummer's coursemates who were doing the Young Officer's Course in Devlali, Ahmednagar and MHOW. This was followed by visits to the NDA and the IMA. The travel was exhausting, but the stories I heard from the people who had been touched by Ummer's life kept me going.

I met Ummer's coursemates—Bhoi, Malik and Ayush in Devlali, Rakesh in MHOW, and Shrey in Pune. I listened to their stories. And I had my own to tell, about meeting his parents and other family members in Kashmir. Each meeting was emotional, and saturated with nostalgia.

'He questioned everything, ma'am,' Malik recalled.

'I'm sure he must be questioning Allah too in heaven,' Bhoi said. Now the people he had left behind were asking the question—why him?

'Ma'am, he was killed on 10 May and we're making a bust of him to be unveiled on the same date at IMA,' Shrey told me.

By then I had done my homework and I corrected him. He was kidnapped on 9 May at 8 p.m. and killed at around 10.30 p.m. on the same night.

'I don't mind, ma'am, if he lives one more day even if it's just on a stone. Let the date be 10th May.'

Chapter 15

The fourth term was the most gruelling of all. In raw cadet terms, they called the fourth-termers 'prostitutes'. But the fourth-termers would often crib that the moniker didn't fit because they didn't get paid for what they were being put through. The cadets were used to training routines at the NDA by now. Even so, they had been forewarned about this term, and the dreaded Camp Rover which loomed before them like an insurmountable obstacle.

Camp Rover would put them through the grind of advanced training in battle subjects like map reading, tent pitching, fitting of web equipment, navigation, endurance training, compass reading and development of leadership skills. Training requires that cadets leave in the night with heavy equipment, perform their tasks and return only in the morning. When morning comes, they are usually ravenous. It is the thought of breakfast that keeps them going in the wee hours, motivating them to finish their navigation on time and reach the field mess located at the other end of camp.

One night, the cadets lost their way and didn't return at the appointed hour. The mess staff were unprepared when they finally turned up, and almost crumbled under the pressure. They could barely keep up with the gargantuan task of serving 300 hungry cadets at once. Bhoi simply declared that he was going to die of hunger and proceeded to stare aimlessly at the sky, frustrated and exhausted at the same time. Although the others were amused, Ummer finally felt sorry for him. He sneaked into the makeshift camp kitchen and spotted some unsupervised boiled eggs. He used his helmet as a basket to carry as many as he could. The boys hadn't noticed Ummer's accomplishment until he came back and crouched on the ground next to them, displaying his treasure. Bhoi and the others attacked instantly, gorging on the stolen eggs.

Hunger temporarily assuaged, they suddenly noticed Rakesh a few steps away, also eating an egg. Ummer, Ayush and Malik walked up to him with raised eyebrows, since Rakesh was a vegetarian. Rakesh's hand stopped mid-air on its way to his mouth. At least he had the grace to look sheepish when caught out.

'Mahatma Gandhi said eggs are vegetarian food,' he blurted out, and the others laughed heartily at the lame excuse.

Drill continued to be Ummer's Waterloo even in the fourth term. Every senior who tried to teach him failed miserably. Trying to compensate for his hopeless performance in drill, he invested extra effort in cycling and swimming. Each step forward was followed by a grand demonstration of his skills in front of his friends. His contagious smile never left his face during these performances.

A month into camp practice, the cadets were on course for completion. The culmination of Camp Rover would be

the 'Josh' run, in which every squadron ran from the camp
to the start point.

Incidentally and most unluckily, the Josh run was on
Bhoi's birthday, which didn't bode well for anyone, let
alone Bhoi.

For one, the run started at night and each cadet in the
squadron was expected to carry a 12 to 13 kg backpack. If
it rained and the rainwater soaked through to the blanket
inside, the pack would weigh a few kilos more, increasing
their burden.

The entire squadron followed a single trail with two
map-readers in front and two at the back. The leaders and
tail-enders were always seniors. One of the leading seniors
held a night-navigation stick with a luminous tape so that
the squadron could follow the light. The senior entrusted
with this task was hardly in an enviable position, as the
stick only added to the weight that he was already carrying.
However, as with all things at the NDA, each individual
has to submit to camp rules and assignments irrespective
of personal preferences, and no one paid much attention
to his woes.

During the run that night, the entire squadron was
spread out over a 200-metre trail when it started to rain.
And sure enough, the backpacks got heavier. One of Bhoi's
backpack straps gave way. There was no way he could have
carried the heavy backpack on one shoulder, and so he had
to stop to fix the broken strap. The other cadets were also
stalled as a result of this. The map-reader finally suggested
that the rest of the squadron move on while Ummer, Malik
and Ayush stayed behind to help Bhoi repair his strap.
They could join the others later on the trail as it was a
straight path ahead. A few other cadets stayed behind with

these boys as they wanted to catch their breath. Rakesh
went ahead with the rest of the team.

Once Bhoi's strap had been fixed, this second team
resumed their walk on the trail mentioned by the senior
map-reader. About 4 or 5 km into it, they realized that
something was amiss. Bhoi, Ayush and Malik had fallen
behind. To make matters worse, they had reached a dead
end. On the left was a steep slope and on the right was
the jungle. Suddenly they froze, hearing a rustling noise
move rapidly towards them through the forest. The next
second, Majid and Rakesh had materialized in the darkness
beside them.

'What are you assholes still doing here?' Majid
demanded, from the top of 1146 peak, visibly furious.

The pair had turned back to find the laggards while all
the other cadets had already reached the top of 1146 peak.
It was the highest peak on the NDA campus.

'But we only did what we were told. We followed the
trail like we were supposed to,' Bhoi lamely reasoned.

'But then you guys were also supposed to change the
trail!' cried Rakesh.

The boys looked at each other, knowing their team
would now be late to finish and lose out on marks because
of their mistakes. They needed a quick solution. Walking
back 5 km to the assigned trail diversion would be the easier
option, but it would take much longer than what they were
now contemplating. They decided that they would climb
the hill, going up the steep side.

The surface was slippery from the rain. Ayush, Ummer
and others managed to make some progress by holding
on to tufts of grass growing on the hillside. But Bhoi and
Malik were lagging behind, and found that the grass, with

roots soft from the rains, had given way when the guys ahead had pulled at them.

Just as they were about to reach the peak, both Malik and Bhoi slipped. They hung precariously over a steep drop, holding on to the branch of a tree that would snap at any moment. Ever resourceful, Majid slid his navigation stick into a fork of the tree that was close enough for the pair to reach. In one swift moment, both shifted to the navigation stick before the branch they were holding on to went crashing down.

'I hope I don't die on my birthday. That would be so tragic for my parents,' Bhoi cried.

'Your birthday seems to be cursed for all of us,' said Malik.

They held on for dear life for a precarious ten minutes that felt like a lifetime. Bhoi started to silently pray. Malik perceived that there was a more pressing matter at hand. The stick was tilted more towards Bhoi as he was the heavier of the two. So Malik asked him to move closer, to take the excess weight off one side. Paralysed with fear, Bhoi refused to budge.

Malik had no choice but to spell out the stark reality. 'Bhoi, the fall from here is steep, straight into the valley below. If the stick breaks, we'll drop like potatoes. And then the only way to rescue us will be to send choppers and the forest below is so dense they may not find us in time. So shift a little Bhoi, please,' he cajoled.

It was a horrible silence for Bhoi as he weighed Malik's words. Then he mustered some courage from the depths of his being and slowly inched closer to Malik.

Shortly, Ummer came down with a safety belt around his waist to rescue them. Malik and Bhoi made their way up the safety rope one after the other and were finally hoisted to the top of the peak. Both were trembling from the experience.

'Phew! That was a close shave. I thought I was going to die today, Ummer. I even had flashes of my picture up in the motivation corner,' Bhoi panted.

'I wouldn't have let you die, Halwai,' said Ummer, patting his back and offering him some water to drink.

* * *

Fourth term was the last term for horse-riding. From the fifth term on, only the good riders or polo players continued to ride. Although relieved that this would be his last term riding, Ummer was also nervous about the lane-jumping test that marked the end of the riding course.

Lane-jumping involves five planks of wood placed one after the other at intervals. In fact, they are more like logs than fancy planks. On the ustad's whistle, the mounted cadets set off and get their horses to jump over all five planks on a canter. Hoisting themselves off their saddle before each jump is key, as it helps them retain their balance on the leap and stay on the horse.

Rakesh was a good rider and cleared the test in one go. Ummer, on the other hand, hadn't quite mastered bottom-lifting, as a result of which he was either precariously on one side of the saddle or kept falling to the front during the jumps. After the fifth log, Ummer flew straight off the front of the horse and fell to the ground. Needless to say, he failed the test.

From then on, he had to take extra classes to pass. In the evenings, when everyone else was resting, Ummer would be sweating it out on horseback.

'Passing the test is one thing. Breaking your neck is a totally different thing,' said Bhoi, clearly concerned for his friend's welfare.

A month before the fourth-term break, Ummer went to Colonel Inderjeet and requested permission to grow his hair. The colonel understood his predicament and gave him special permission right away. Now, when his friends teased him about the extra riding lessons, Ummer would get back at them on Sundays, when they all had to have the compulsory haircut he was exempted from.

Four days short of the term break, by a grand stroke of luck, Ummer managed to pass his riding test. He also managed to go home.

It had been a whole year since his family had seen him. His grandmother had prepared kheer for him. Looking at Ummer relish the kheer, his grandmother asked, 'They don't give you kheer in the NDA?'

'They do, grandma, but it's not like this,' was Ummer's usual reply. Ummer had made sure to buy pens for both his sisters, and they were thrilled to receive him as well as the gifts.

After the happy reunion with his family, all he could think about was Tahzun. He wanted to meet her as soon as he possibly could. But Javed, his partner in crime, wasn't in Kashmir any more; he had moved to Dehradun to complete his graduation. Ummer missed his friend all the more because he was now at his wits' end, wondering how he could meet Tahzun without Javed's ingenious help in plotting the rendezvous.

But where there is a will, there is a way! Ummer managed to convince a friend of Tahzun's to help him meet her at the same place as the last time. When he met them both, Ummer opened his bag and took out a pair of jeans. A gift for her friend, he said. Tahzun was overcome with jealousy that was written all over her face. Ummer loved to see that expression on her face.

'Don't worry! I've got one for you also,' Ummer said teasingly.

Tahzun smiled. He gifted her the jeans, but Tahzun now wanted the pair that Ummer was wearing.

'Now?' It was Ummer's turn to be shocked.

'Yes!' Nuzhat, Tahzun's friend, teasingly insisted.

Ummer didn't hesitate. He stood up and removed his jeans. Tahzun shrieked and covered her eyes.

'How can you, Ummer? Absolutely shameless,' she complained, her hands still over her eyes.

Ummer swiftly grabbed the jeans that he had bought for her and put them on. They shared the same waist size.

'The NDA does that to you. I have zero inhibitions now,' said Ummer as he nonchalantly zipped them on.

'Here,' she said simply, handing him a gift.

Ummer wasn't expecting this at all, and didn't know how to react when he opened it to see a Casio watch. He had always wanted a watch like this one, and he knew Tahzun must have saved every penny of her pocket money for months and then some more to buy him this gift.

They were quiet for a while. Tahzun was happy, just basking in the expression on Ummer's face that told her he loved the watch and was very touched by her gift.

'You shouldn't have . . .' he started to say, but she shushed him and changed the topic.

'I kept checking your FB profile when I missed you and couldn't speak with you. Why have you put up Holi and Diwali celebration pictures? You know how people will react here!'

Tahzun was a sensitive girl, keenly aware of the attitudes and prejudices of the people around her.

'All those boys celebrated Eid with me, so why wouldn't I celebrate their festivals?' Ummer asked, innocently perplexed. The training in NDA was now showing in Ummer's attitude. He had been away for four years now, and didn't realize that the situation in Kashmir had taken a turn for the worse. There were elements in the Valley that reacted violently to any display of tolerance or leaning towards secularism.

At this point, Ummer began to wonder how people could be so narrow-minded. He even told Tahzun that he didn't know if it was safe for him to live in Kashmir after he was commissioned. On the other hand, he also wondered if the situation was so bad that he would have to leave the army. He loved his home and he loved the army. Choosing between the two was not something that his heart would even consider an option.

Tahzun could only tell him not to worry and to keep a low profile while he was at home.

The next day, Ummer visited his old school and met some of his juniors. They were all excited to see him and told him they were working hard to clear the UPSC exam. One of them was preparing to take it again as he didn't pass the exam on his first attempt. But he said his parents were not pleased with his decision, as they believed that the army does not practise religious tolerance and would not let him go to the masjid for namaz on Fridays.

'Ummer bhai, do they let you go to the masjid on Fridays?' The boy asked.

Ummer didn't have an answer as he had never gone to the masjid in all his time at the NDA.

Ummer also discussed his sisters' education with his father on that trip. He requested his father to send the girls out of the state for further studies. He felt that if Asmat and Usma moved out, it would eventually be easier to shift his parents and the rest of the family too. Leaving the army was not an option, but he wanted his family out of harm's way. And the only way he could envisage them all living safely was if they built a life outside Kashmir.

With these thoughts weighing his mind down, Ummer left for Pune for the last year of his training at the NDA.

Ummer's leg still gave him trouble, although it was slightly better. He was hoping it would hold up as the fifth term started with cross-country.

A few weeks into the new term, Ummer was appointed sergeant, a position that held some weight in the academy. And one of the first initiatives he took in his new role as a leader was to talk to the seniors about securing permission for namaz on Fridays.

The room went silent when Ummer brought up the topic. It was simply unprecedented. All Muslim cadets observed roza during the holy month, but none had asked for permission to go to the mosque to pray on Fridays. Even cadets from Islamic countries like Tajikistan had never made such an appeal. Nevertheless, the seniors did communicate the request to the officers.

Major Rakesh Singh, who was also the counsellor for the Delta Squadron, was the officer they approached. He clearly needed some time to mull over it as he didn't discuss the matter further with them that day. However, the very next morning, he addressed the entire squadron.

'How many of you would like to attend namaz on Fridays? Let's have a show of hands,' he said, raising his right hand.

There were many cadets who wanted to go if they could, but they had debated for a few hours the previous evening on whether it was a legitimate demand, considering it fairly from all possible angles. Some were quick to point out that the Christian cadets could then ask for permission to visit the church on Sundays. And the Hindus could no doubt request permission to observe their rites every day of the week, as they had a plethora of gods and goddesses.

The Muslim cadets knew that their first and foremost duty as soldiers was to their nation. In spite of this knowledge, they put up a reluctant hand that day.

For Ummer, this was about more than just offering prayers on Fridays. He wanted to go back home and tell his people that their religious beliefs were accepted and supported by the academy and the army. One of the major contentions of some Kashmiris who sympathized with the radicals was that the rest of India and the army didn't care for their religion. For Ummer himself, it wasn't important to pray five times a day. He hadn't done that in years. But he did want to be able to tell his juniors back home truthfully that joining the army would not involve sacrificing their religious sentiments and observances. However, only he knew that was the real reason for his bringing up the Friday namaz proposal.

'And who is the leader who initiated this?' asked Major Rakesh.

Ummer's hand stayed up while the rest lowered theirs. Realizing that he hadn't spoken up, he shouted, stepping forward from his row, 'It's me, sir.'

Major Rakesh appeared to size him up for a fleeting moment that only Ummer caught.

'You'll be in charge of the Friday namaz then. Take a checklist from me later today,' the major said.

'Yes sir,' Ummer responded. He wasn't expecting it to be easy. Taking complete responsibility for the cadets who would be joining the namaz was going to be an additional burden that term, but it was a price he would willingly pay.

Ummer had a uniform approved for the namaz by Major Rakesh: muftis with khaki-coloured pants and a full-sleeved shirt. On returning from the masjid each Friday, they were all to change into their games rig. During the weeks that followed, and for as long as he was namaz-in-charge at the NDA, Ummer made sure that the discipline of the NDA was never compromised by the cadets' attendance of Friday prayers.

The namaz initiative was a milestone in the history of Muslim cadets at the NDA. The happiest of the lot were the cadets from Tajikistan as they could now offer their long-suspended Friday prayers.

Ummer's stubborn nature had often landed him in trouble in the past, but he was now channelling this trait towards more positive causes.

Firing of Light Machine Guns (LMG) is taught in the fifth term. The drill involves five battalions, each consisting of four squadrons. During one of the practice sessions, the third battalion had somehow managed to lose a cartridge.

In cahoots with the second battalion, they decided not to report the matter to anyone.

However, the NDA has stringent rules regarding ammunition used in training. It is the rule that cartridges be counted after firing practice so that there is an account of the number of bullets fired. As the third battalion was leaving, Ummer noticed that a cartridge was missing and objected vehemently. But he was up against the second and third battalions, who were determined not to report the loss as they would have to spend the entire night searching for the missing cartridge case. Shrey Avasthi was in the second battalion. Although his initial urge was to punch Ummer in the face and ask him to shut up, he couldn't help but be impressed by his friend's stance as he stood his ground against two whole battalions. So he decided to take Ummer's side.

It looked like a brawl would break out any second, as the second battalion inched threateningly towards Ummer and one of the cadets went so far as to seize him by the collar. Out of nowhere, Bhoi appeared and stood between Ummer and his adversaries.

'Stop it! What are you guys doing?' he shouted in his most menacing voice.

'Ah, the mother cow has come to save its calf,' they taunted. Unflinching, Bhoi stared them down as hard as he could.

'Let's find the cartridge and be done with it,' Shrey said, trying to defuse the situation.

The battalion looked at Ummer and saw that he wasn't going to back down. With many a swear word aimed at him, they proceeded to look for the missing case. An hour later, it was Shrey who found the cartridge.

When the second and third battalions eventually handed the case over to the authorities, they were told in no uncertain terms that they had had a narrow escape from one of the worst offences they could commit in the NDA.

'It's a good thing you looked for it and brought it back. If you hadn't returned it or reported it, the NDA would have turned into a tandoor and you lot would have become roasted tandoori chicken by tomorrow,' was the officer's mild response.

Power, discipline and accountability go hand in hand. Ummer was learning to exercise all three from the core of his being.

One evening, he was taking a break and surfing channels in the anteroom when a news flash announced the floods in Kashmir. Alarmed, he ran up the flight of stairs to his dorm. Ayush noticed that Ummer looked unusually stressed.

'What happened?' he asked.

It took all of Ummer's steely resolve to not lose his cool at this moment.

'I need to call home,' he said, tersely.

The two boys rushed to the phone booth and Ummer frantically dialled home—first his family, and then everyone he knew. He couldn't get through to a single person. Even an automated voice message telling him that the line was busy would have been comforting at this stage. Instead, it was a blank line for every call.

Ayush couldn't contain himself any longer. 'What happened, Ummer?' he asked again.

'There are floods in Kashmir. Over two thousand villages have been affected. Evacuation is under progress, and I'm worried to death about my family.'

For the next few days, Ummer was exempted from all his normal routines at the NDA. He sat by the phone booth all day, and kept dialling every number he had. This went on for days, and soon everyone at the academy knew and sympathized with Ummer.

After almost a week, the mobile network was up and running again in Kashmir, and Ummer finally heard a dial tone on his father's mobile.

His heart thumped hard against his chest while he waited for someone to answer.

'Hello Sahibji, we are all fine. We knew that you would be worried.' It was Usma.

'How are you all?' he screamed, as if nothing Usma said had registered.

'We are fine, Sahibji. The floods washed away our fields, but all of us are fine,' she reiterated.

'You are fine? Ammi, Abbu and everyone else is fine?'

'We are all fine, Sahibji. Please don't worry about us,' said Usma for what felt like the hundredth time.

After speaking with the rest of his family, he hung up and hugged Bhoi who had accompanied him to the phone booth.

All the boys had rallied around him these past few days. Whenever they could, they would go sit with him at the booth, or trawl the Internet for the latest news updates. Even the rest of the squadron were worried for him and would often ask each other if Ummer had had any luck getting through to his parents on the phone.

As for Ummer, he finally slept soundly that night, exhaustion knocking him out as soon as he hit the bed.

The next morning at cross-country, he ran like a man possessed. It could have been guilt over having been exempted from the routine of the academy for the past week or just sheer relief, but he ran like the wind was carrying his feet.

Although they missed him terribly, his family forbade him from visiting them during his fifth term break as well. The situation in the Valley was tense again. He was asked to stay with his uncle in Delhi instead. The month-long break did Ummer good, however, and he returned to the academy, refreshed and ready for his sixth term.

It seemed like the next five months passed in a blur. Before they knew it, it was time for their passing-out parade.

The floods had taken their toll and the Valley was slowly recovering from the ensuing devastation. Communication lines were still down, and in this general state of disarray, Ummer's parents could not make it to their son's passing-out parade.

Ummer was eternally grateful, however, that his uncle from Delhi could come down to Pune and attend the ceremony. It was a proud moment for all cadets who had successfully completed three years of rigorous training and their parents and relatives. The passing-out parade was like the ultimate culmination of rigorous training the boys had gone through to become men. The values of an officer were ingrained in them irrespective of the services they chose.

The cadets were expected to showcase a drill that was supposed to be the bedrock of discipline and with everyone in sync, it instilled a sense of martial discipline.

Uncle Rahmat, sitting on the stands along with the other parents and relatives, wondered where his nephew was when bugles sounded the call and the gates of the Quarter Master Fort opened. A stream of smartly turned-out young cadets from all services began to fill the Khetarpal Drill Square, named after Lieutenant Khetarpal who had made the supreme sacrifice and had been awarded the Param Vir Chakra in the 1971 Indo–Pak War.

The synchronized drill was a treat to watch, but the fog did some damage on that day (28 November 2015). Ummer, still not perfect at the drill, managed somehow and the fog helped as no one could notice if he did go wrong.

After the drill, the passing-out cadets went past the quarter deck in a slow march with an air force flypast in the sky carried out by fighter jets flown over the Drill Square. It was a spectacular event that instilled a feeling of achievement and pride in every cadet.

The cadets could not leave the academy without paying their respects to those killed in action. On the day of the parade, all the cadets paid tribute to the war heroes in the Hut of Remembrance. The names of all the NDA cadets who have been killed in action have been immortalized and enshrined in gold on black marble. It was after three years of rigorous training that every cadet became aware of the concept: sacrifice for the country. History sometimes can be a cruel companion of soldiers. At the ceremony, every cadet in the academy was inspired to honour those dead soldiers who made their great institution proud.

The cadets marched to the beat of the drums commemorating the end of the three memorable years spent at the NDA. They were all looking forward to a new beginning, turning from boys into men—men of honour.

A month later, Ummer and his coursemates joined the Indian Military Academy (IMA), Dehradun, while those joining the navy went to Ezimala in Kerala and the air force cadets went to Dindigul in Tamil Nadu for the completion of their training. From just 'cadets' in the NDA, they had now graduated to being called 'gentleman cadets' in the IMA. After having spent three years together in the NDA, they had developed a camaraderie that would last for the rest of their lives, irrespective of the services they joined. For cadets from the NDA, the IMA was a cakewalk and they were ready to face its challenges head-on.

Ummer was delighted to find himself sharing a room with Shrey Avasthi at the IMA. One day, Shrey brought up the topic of Burhan Wani.

'Is he from your town?' he asked Ummer.

'No, he is from Tral.'

'Ummer, have you really attended a jihadi camp?'

Ummer stared at Shrey for a moment, quite shocked. Then he noticed the naughty smile on his friend's face and understood it was just a joke.

'I'm only asking because you are so good with tactics in the camps. It makes me suspect that you have attended both sides of the training,' said Shrey enviously before he burst into laughter.

Ummer realized that the brat was giving him a compliment and laughed too.

'Burhan Wani has taken the Valley by storm. He's being hailed as the new hero of Kashmir,' said Ummer.

Shrey wanted to hear what Ummer had to say about Wani, as they were both from Kashmir and about the same age, and yet had made such radically different life choices.

'Burhan is seen as a messiah, someone who fights for the rights of the people of Kashmir. So he's perceived more as a revolutionary on the lines of Bhagat Singh, than as a terrorist.'

'But Bhagat Singh was fighting for India while Burhan is fighting against India, against his own people and against his own government,' snorted Shrey in protest.

'It's not quite as black and white as that. You haven't lived in Kashmir; you don't feel the frustration of the youth who grow up in the Valley.'

As they were deep in discussion, a bunch of other cadets joined them. 'But Ummer, you and Burhan share the same history. Both of you were manhandled by security forces while you were young, but you chose to be part of the solution. Whereas Burhan went on to become part of the problem. Kashmiris should be following you, not him! Your journey should be a source of inspiration for them. Burhan is just a coward, and he's simply asking to be caught and killed by the armed forces one of these days.'

The others all chimed in with Shrey's words.

For the first time in his life, Ummer felt a deep sense of peace and fulfilment with regard to the choices he had made so far. True appreciation is precious when it comes from your own kind. And by now Ummer realized that his 'kind', in the truest sense, was the Indian Army.

Shrey's words of encouragement motivated Ummer to strive to excel in every activity at the IMA. He worked doubly hard on his weaknesses, including drill. He put in so much practice that the results began to show. Soon, the drill instructor moved him to the first row for the upcoming passing-out parade. By now, Ummer had also overcome his other Achilles heel. He was riding his bike like a pro.

The IMA training lasted for a year. Javed happened to be completing his graduation in Dehradun at the same time. During 'liberties', when Ummer was allowed to go outside campus, he often met up with his old friend and the pair would watch movies together.

The one piece of advice that Ummer gave Javed during those days was not to contest the perception that the rest of India had of militancy in the Valley. Burhan Wani was the emerging face of Kashmiri terrorism. A sizeable chunk of the Kashmiri youth were big aficionados of the brand of militant nationalism he represented, and took to social media to defend Wani's actions to the world. However, the rest of the country saw him as a terrorist who had resorted to unconstitutional means to fulfil illegitimate demands.

At the same time, in conversations with his friends at the IMA, Ummer managed to present a more rational view of the problems of the people in the Valley. As a Kashmiri training to become an officer in the army, he was developing a unique perspective on the conditions back home, that of an objective insider.

In July 2016, security forces finally gunned Burhan Wani down in a terrorist encounter. Shrey's prophecy had come true. The Valley erupted with protests, and a curfew was imposed that lasted fifty-three days. In the mayhem that followed the death of Wani, ninety-six people died.

Ummer's family was getting paranoid, as young people were dying every day in the Valley, in ever greater numbers. So Ummer had no choice but to forgo another vacation at home, and visit his uncle and his childhood friend Zainub in Delhi instead.

The one saving grace of this vacation in exile was that Ummer finally got to see India Gate on an outing with Zainub. He instantly felt connected to the Amar Jawan Jyoti or the Flame of the Immortal Soldier, perhaps because it reminded him of his visits to the Hut of Remembrance at the NDA. The boys sat in reverence before the flame for a while, each updating the other on their lives. Soon after, Ummer left Delhi for his final term at the IMA.

Before Ummer could pass out, he had to choose an 'arm'. The combat arms directly engage with the enemy in actual combat and include the Infantry, the Armoured Corps and others. The supporting arms like the Corps of Engineers and Signals support the combat arms. Then there are the Services like the Education Corps, Ordnance Corps and others who provide logistical support.

Cadets usually seek advice from friends and family in the armed forces before they make their choice. Since Ummer didn't have a single relative in the army, he called Lieutenant Colonel Inderjeet Singh. The colonel advised Ummer against the Jammu & Kashmir Light Infantry (JAK LI) even though its regimental centre was in Ummer's home state. Most of the troops in this regiment are Muslims while the rest are from other Kashmiri ethnic groups.

Ummer had really wanted to serve in his state while also being closer to his family. But that wasn't to be. However, he was eventually selected for 2 Raj Rif, one of the oldest and most decorated infantry units of the Indian Army.

Ummer's drill ustad was all praises for the unit and Ummer himself was convinced that he was on the right track.

'Will I ever be able to serve in Kashmir, ustad?' Ummer asked wistfully.

'Oh, the unit has served in Kashmir more than anywhere else. Don't worry about it.'

The ustad was proud that the cadet he had trained would soon be part of such a legendary unit. As for Ummer, having made up his mind, he called all his former instructors to inform them that he was about to be commissioned as a 2 Raj Rif officer for life.

By now Ummer could ride a bicycle with full control and ride a horse like a champion. At the end of the four years of training, he was a transformed being. In a way, he felt proud of his little achievements and would often showcase his talent to his friends.

'See Bhoi, I can ride it with no hands,' Ummer would shout, showing off to Bhoi.

Before they knew it, the year came to an end and they were ready for another passing out, only this time they were going to be commissioned officers after that.

The passing-out parade of the IMA is a grand affair, and Ummer had really wanted his parents to be with him in his finest hour. But due to the ongoing turmoil over Burhan Wani's death, his parents could barely step out of their own home, leave alone Kashmir.

Zainub and Javed made it, however, and although Ummer missed his parents terribly, he was grateful to have his two best friends by his side on this very important day.

In many ways, the passing-out parade at the IMA was similar to the NDA one, but this time Ummer was adept at drill and stood in the first row of his squadron. Only the best make it to that row. It only showed that Ummer was clearly not the type to give up.

The drill culminated at the 'Antim Pag', which was literally a plaque with the words 'Antim Pag' meaning 'final step' engraved on it. It was symbolic in terms of the men now becoming officers.

The piping ceremony was done by Ummer's friends who removed the flaps from his shoulders that were covering the two shining stars. His friends looked at them with awe. Gentleman Cadet Ummer Fayaz was now Lieutenant Ummer Fayaz. He was now going to embark on the path he had chosen for himself after taking an oath to protect the nation.

The adjutant of the academy read the oath in the presence of the four holy books placed in front of him while all the cadets repeated after him. The oath gave goosebumps not only to the cadets but also to the parents and guests:

'I hereby solemnly swear that I will bear true faith and allegiance to the Constitution of India, as by law established and that I will, as in duty bound honestly and faithfully, serve in the regular army of the Union of India and go wherever ordered, by land, sea or air, and that I will observe and obey all the commands of the President of the Union of India and the commands of any officer set above me, even to the peril of my life.'

Soon after the ceremony, Ummer left for Kashmir and visited his home briefly before he joined the 2 Raj Rif centre in Delhi for the formal induction into his unit. Just a few weeks after induction, Ummer joined his unit at Akhnoor, near the LoC in Jammu.

Chapter 16

After completing their military training, cadets are more often than not raring to go on the battlefield. It is often said in jest that they are even more eager to pick up their arms against enemies than to kiss the girls they have left behind. Ummer was no different. Academy training is geared towards prepping cadets for combat in the spirit of serving the nation. And the best opportunity for a young officer to fulfil his calling is a posting at the borders, where he can exercise his prerogative to protect his country from an enemy breach or infiltration.

The commanding officer of 2 Raj Rif, Colonel Rohit Patil, was already tracking every move of Lieutenant Ummer Fayaz, the latest recruit to his unit. He was informed when Ummer reported at the Jammu transit camp, and knew that he had taken the Poonch convoy. At the Poonch transit camp, he was picked up by his unit and driven to the Akhnoor transit camp. From there, Ummer would have to reach his unit in Kehri.

Colonel Rohit had already done an in-depth analysis of the young officer's strengths and weaknesses over the past four years of training, both at the NDA and the IMA. He knew everything that there was to know about what made this new recruit tick. Lieutenant Ummer Fayaz was deliberately checked at every post to test his patience and tolerance levels. However, unlike in his childhood, Ummer wasn't threatened by this any more, as he felt he was now part of the establishment and had earned it. He was a commissioned officer of the Indian Army and proud of his new identity.

At the Akhnoor Traffic Control Police (TCP) post, Lieutenant Ummer Fayaz was given a bicycle with a few tin cans tied to it, to ride to Kehri. Of course, Ummer was now an expert cyclist. As he cycled towards his destination, he felt that he was on his way to the rest of his life. The tin cans rattled and clanked, as if announcing his hard-won victory to the valleys of Jammu and Kashmir. Here was a boy who had gone through every adversity a Kashmir boy faces while growing up, but instead of blindly revolting against the system, he had become the change he expected to see. His training at the academy had catalysed the transformation process. An entire generation of a Kashmiri family now had the potential to change forever.

Lieutenant Ummer reported at the security gate of his unit where he was received with a volley of salutes. He was then led inside to be given a traditional welcome at the Sarv Dharm Sthal. In units where there isn't enough space to create a place of worship for each religion separately, a Sarv Dharm Sthal is created, which serves as a place of worship for all religions.

All this was very new to Ummer, and he felt quite overwhelmed. But not for a moment did he forget the protocol or his manners. He made sure to pay his respects to all the officers and other important functionaries in his unit. He also met the soldiers, the majority of whom turned out to be either Jats from Haryana or Rajputs from Rajasthan. It suddenly struck him on that first day that he had no cultural or religious affinity with anyone in the entire platoon. At the NDA and the IMA, he always had a few friends who were either Muslim or had some previous Kashmiri connection.

He had introduced himself to the entire unit before he had a chance to meet his CO, Colonel Rohit.

'Welcome to 2 Raj Rif, Lieutenant Ummer Fayaz!' Colonel Rohit greeted Ummer.

Colonel Rohit's demeanour exuded warmth, and Ummer was already feeling less intimidated. Over tea, the colonel had a chat with him and plied him with personal and professional questions. He already knew a great deal about Lieutenant Ummer's life, but wanted to corroborate the facts and details. As the CO, it was his duty to get to know his baby officer. The most junior officer was considered the baby of the unit, and so Ummer would literally be treated with kid gloves in the beginning.

In no time at all, Ummer became a part of the unit. He spent every waking hour with his fellow-soldiers, and it was only natural that he soon felt a sense of belonging. The men, in turn, loved him because he was young, extremely adaptive and an excellent sportsman. Again, the discipline as well as the sense of community that the academy had instilled, helped Ummer blend in.

The pre-induction training in terrain and war tactics gave him a whole new perspective on combat. Although he had been put through the grind at the academy, this was palpably different as it was a real war zone with real enemies. A single mistake could actually endanger or end lives, and as an officer, Ummer would be responsible for many lives.

Ummer did extremely well in his pre-induction test, and was now ready to take over a post at the LoC along with ten men. The day he was to begin, a senior JCO issued a weapon to Ummer—an AK-47. He took the gun in his hands with mixed feelings. A part of him was revelling in the might of it. But he also knew the burden of responsibility that came with it. Unlike the drill weapons he was used to handling, this one could prove lethal.

Ummer felt a strange sense of reverence and instinctively touched the gun to his forehead like he would an object of religious importance. He then swung it across his left shoulder to see how it felt. Growing up, he had witnessed many young boys in his hometown who had taken the path of militancy show off their Kalashnikovs (AKs). But Ummer hoped, with his gun, to mark the difference—between right and wrong, legitimate and illegitimate, constitutional and unconstitutional, moral and immoral, and above all, the difference between love and hate.

Colonel Rohit had a brief meeting with him before he left for the post. 'That post is now your masjid. And the welfare of those men and the security of your country is now your religion. All the best, Lieutenant Ummer Fayaz!'

'Thank you, sir!' Ummer shouted as he saluted his CO.

The area of his post was clearly demarcated, and their task would be to guard against infiltration and movement of terrorists. There were ten men on Ummer's team who were paired into five groups. Ummer himself was paired with Naik Amit Kumar Teotia, a Jat from Meerut. Amit was his operational buddy. Whenever Ummer went out to patrol or check the fence, Amit went with him. Ummer was the only officer on the team, and that inevitably designated him as its leader.

One day, at around 2300 hrs, Ummer called Tahzun. Between his busy schedule and the non-existent network connectivity at the border, Ummer was barely able to keep in touch with his loved ones. But somehow, every time he tried Tahzun, he always seemed to get through to her.

'How are you?' Tahzun asked in a low, trembling voice.

Tahzun was aware that Ummer was at the border, and she worried endlessly. All the violence and devastation she had already seen around her did not make her immune to anxiety on Ummer's behalf.

'I love you, Tahzun,' Ummer said simply, in response. It was the first time he had said those words. Somehow, on this day, he didn't feel vulnerable about wearing his heart on his sleeve. On the contrary, the words sounded just right.

Tahzun was silent, evidently too shy to respond. Just then, she heard gunshots in the background.

'I'll call you back. There seems to be a problem,' said Ummer's eerily calm voice that was far from reassuring for Tahzun at that point.

His first step was to gather his team together to assess the situation. He was informed by the men that the Pakistan Army had violated the ceasefire agreement. The senior JCO called the company commander who in turn informed the CO. Minute by minute, the firing got heavier, and Colonel Rohit gave standing orders for retaliation.

The team took position behind a big rock, waiting with bated breath. After the initial volley that lasted a few minutes, the firing stopped. Then Ummer decided to take a step forward to gauge the situation. But the moment he became visible to the enemy, the firing resumed with a vengeance. Amit pulled him back down and Ummer hit his back against the rock with a thud.

'Saab, be careful! A bullet has no address. If it lands on you, it *will* kill you,' said Amit. Ummer nodded in agreement.

Ironically, it was the most exciting day of Ummer's life. He had confessed his love to Tahzun. And almost immediately after, he was also thrust into a battle zone, where all his training looked him in the eye as if to test his mettle.

Strangely, he felt calm. And just as they began to feel that they were safe, a bullet came whizzing over their heads, hitting the rock just above Amit's helmet. The entire team ducked.

'On a crawl, let's take cover behind those individual rocks one by one. I'll take the lead and give cover,' Ummer commanded.

He crawled forward, took cover behind one of the biggest rocks, and started firing. He gestured to the men, sending them on crawls in different directions to dodge the enemy. But the firing was relentless and came at them from all sides.

After several hours of some generous burning of ammunition on both sides, finally, there was silence. Ummer looked down at his wrist to check Tahzun's watch. It was a little past midnight, but he decided they would guard the post for a few more hours.

As dawn was breaking, the team returned to their post, bone-weary and sleep-deprived. Ummer grinned at Amit. Despite the physical exhaustion, Ummer experienced, for the first time, the euphoria of having defended his nation from an assault.

'Saab, today you lost your virginity,' Amit said, referring to Ummer's first taste of the enemy on the field.

'But tell me, what was the thrill in this? They fired. We fired. And then it all stopped.'

'Before long, it will start all over again. You see, Saab, they have to keep the conflict alive. How else would they justify the need for a gargantuan defence budget to the people of Pakistan? The army in Pakistan live like kings and have to keep up their lavish lifestyles. They create an imaginary enemy by provoking us to fire, so that they can tell their people that there is a real threat. That is the only way for them to flourish.'

Ummer immediately drew a mental parallel to the situation in Kashmir. Of course! It all made sense now.

After that first taste of combat, Ummer was always on the alert subconsciously. He understood that life in the army, and especially on the LoC, was anything but predictable.

He couldn't get through to Tahzun to reassure her of his safety as there was no mobile network at the post for the next few days. So he simply had to hope that she knew he was all right.

The food cooked on the lines was usually dal-baati, a Rajasthani staple. Ummer liked to try new food, but none of it ever usurped his undying love for rice and dal. On occasion, the cook would prepare some of Ummer's favourite dishes for a change.

Before he knew it, two months had passed since his arrival at the post and a new assignment came his way. Colonel Rohit was growing concerned about the SO 66 Alpha post. He knew that, once the monsoons arrived, it would only be a matter of time before a flash flood swept it all away. But he felt they might have time to salvage the situation if they hurried.

He summoned the baby of the unit, Ummer, and handed the task to him.

'We need to rebuild SO 66 Alpha. It's concrete, and needs to be broken down before it can be rebuilt. We don't have too much time on our hands before the monsoons arrive, so make sure the men work double-time to complete the task.'

Ummer was determined not to let Colonel Rohit down. His team got to work immediately, hammering away at the concrete blocks of SO 66 Alpha. Their instructions were to break the existing post and build one underground. It was going to be one hell of a task!

One evening, someone discovered the phone network was back, and the entire team rejoiced. Ummer called home and spoke at length to his parents and sisters. He even called up his aunts and uncles, paternal and maternal. During one of these conversations, he was delighted to hear from his maternal uncle that his cousin Musrat was engaged and would get married soon. Ummer just didn't want to miss this wedding!

'Mama, I really want to be there for Musrat's wedding. Is there any way you can postpone the date?'

Ummer knew he had to finish building the post before he could even ask his CO for leave.

'Of course, Sahibji! You let me know when you can come home, and we'll celebrate her wedding only when you are here with us.'

'Mama, I hope the boy is good enough for Musrat?' Ummer inquired.

'Yes, Sahibji! We don't have any boys, so we are looking forward to welcoming a son into the family. He will be living with us after the wedding. The boy is kind and intelligent.'

Uncle Maqbool sounded very convinced of the choice, and Ummer was reassured that Musrat would be happy.

'Very happy to hear that, Mama. I'll see you soon then.'

Ummer was about to hang up when Maqbool said, 'But Sahibji, where are you and what are you doing? We never get through to your phone.'

'Mama jaan, I can't tell you anything on the phone. I will call you soon to inform you of the dates. I'm fine, don't worry about me.'

Despite being at the border among complete strangers, Ummer felt much safer at his post than he did when he visited his home. He had absolute faith in the men who soldiered with him and knew that they had his back, no matter what.

Maqbool hesitated for a moment, but felt it was imperative to caution his beloved nephew.

'The situation here is tense, Sahibji. I hate to say this, but I would really advise you not to come,' he said, the pain in his voice evident.

'Musrat is my sister, Mama. If I don't come for her wedding, what sort of brother am I? Moreover, I am also getting a brother in her fiancé, and it is my duty as a brother to make sure he settles in well. And for how long will I run, Mama? Kashmir is home. With all of you there, can I stay away forever?'

There was nothing Maqbool could say to that. He was a simple man whose only wish was for his family to be safe and happy. He hung up with a troubled heart.

Ummer and his team toiled like men possessed for an entire month. And on 22 April 2017, Ummer reported to Colonel Rohit, beaming at having completed the task. He was also able to ask for leave. Colonel Rohit was very proud of his young officer and knew that it would be a well-deserved break.

'So, first leave, Ummer?' the colonel asked.

'Yes sir! My cousin's wedding, sir.' Ummer smiled.

'Before you leave, I want to give you a task.'

As a commanding officer, Colonel Rohit knew how to get the maximum out of his men in minimum time.

'I want you to arrange the books in the library according to their genres,' Colonel Rohit said pointing to the cupboards containing books that showed no order in their display.

It was through these small tasks that senior officers taught new recruits the importance of paperwork, classification and time management.

It was evening when Ummer received the order from his CO, so he sat down right after dinner to arrange the books. He skimmed through or read the blurb on the back cover of every book before classifying and grouping them as fiction, non-fiction, children's literature, military or journals. There were over 700 books in the library. By 3 a.m., Ummer had arranged all of them according to genre. Then, he joined an early morning convoy at 5 a.m. to reach the nearest bus stand. Needless to say, as soon as he boarded the bus, he slept like a baby.

Colonel Rohit was very impressed with Ummer's work in the library. 'When did Saab sleep last night?' he asked the senior JCO, knowing that Ummer must have been up all night to complete this Herculean task.

'Saab didn't sleep, Shriman,' the JCO confirmed.

'How was his performance at the post?' The colonel wanted to know more about his boy.

'Shriman, Ummer Saab is different. He doesn't discriminate. In fact, we kept telling him that he is our Saab, but he didn't just give orders. He worked as hard as we did while hammering the old post down. And then he lifted every stone along with us to make that post.'

The JCO had only good things to say about Ummer. Colonel Rohit was pleased to hear about his performance at the post, but it was his commitment to smaller, less glorious tasks such as the library job that proved Ummer's true worth to him. The CO was satisfied that Ummer's recruitment had reinforced the unit's reputation.

After they had last spoken, Tahzun tried every day to get through to Ummer's mobile, but she had no luck. At first, she was sad. Then a mixture of grief and anxiety made her very angry indeed. Love truly has many expressions! When the CO sanctioned his leave, Ummer was bursting to tell her the news. But Tahzun was so upset with him that she didn't pick up his call.

Ever full of mischief and surprises, Ummer instructed Uncle Maqbool to keep his homecoming a secret. When he reached Anantnag, his family couldn't have been more astonished or overjoyed.

Tahzun still wasn't picking up his calls, but Ummer knew that she would come around. Sure enough, when she learnt that Ummer was in Kashmir, all her anger dissipated and she called him in a worried frenzy.

Ummer's mobile flashed her name. Relieved and ecstatic, he immediately answered the call.

'Why the hell did you have to come here?' she yelled. Confused at first, he checked whether it was really her calling.

'To meet *you*, jaan!' Ummer said softly.

'Ummer, you know the situation here. You really shouldn't have come.'

Ummer was relieved. So she still did love him. For a few days, he had worried that she was so angry she probably never wanted to see him again.

But Tahzun could not have been more in love with him or more anxious about him than she was at that moment. The situation in Kashmir had deteriorated irreversibly since their childhood and adolescence. Tolerance levels were now at an all-time low. Lives were cheap. She didn't know how to get him to understand the darkness that was engulfing the Valley.

'Musrat is my sister, Tahzun. I'm the only brother she has. I have responsibilities towards my family too.

How long can I run from my home, from my own people, and from you? I'll have to face everything one day. I'd rather it be sooner than later,' Ummer said calmly.

Tahzun was weeping uncontrollably. Unable to speak, she hung up on him.

Asmat was already home, waiting excitedly for Usma to come to Kulgam from Anantnag for the wedding. But Ummer insisted on going several days ahead to Uncle Maqbool's in Batpora, to lend a hand for the wedding preparations.

'Papa, I'm leaving for Batpora with Ammi tomorrow. Uncle Maqbool will need help,' Ummer told Fayaz.

'You will visit them and eat ten kilos of chicken and twenty kilos of rice and dal on a daily basis. That would be anyone's yearly ration. I don't know where all that food goes,' Fayaz jested, trying to conceal the fact that he didn't want his son to leave so soon after he had arrived.

Jameela bestowed Fayaz with a nasty look and started to give him a piece of her mind. Ummer looked indulgently at his parents sparring over him while he packed.

'You're packing as if you're the groom. What will you do with so many clothes?'

Ummer smiled. He couldn't tell his father that he was going to meet Tahzun after the wedding. He had a lot of making up to do with her.

On 8 May 2017, Ummer gave the watch that Tahzun had given him to the local repair shop. The battery had died. The shopkeeper said he would get a new battery and give it back to him in four days.

On the same day, Ummer and Jameela were greeted by Uncle Maqbool's family with much love and the boisterous warmth peculiar to all family celebrations. Maqbool told Jameela that it finally felt like a wedding with both of them over.

His cousins were all over him and didn't let him out of their sight for even a second. As they crowded around him, he took gifts out of his bag for Musrat, Suby, Iqra and Anista. Musrat received more gifts than the others as she was the bride.

Uncle Maqbool was keeping the wedding low-key and he just wanted everyone to give their blessings to the young couple.

'This is where you were born, Ummer,' Jameela told her son, her voice brimming over with nostalgia. Ummer hugged his mother and kissed her. He was wanted everywhere, but he wanted, above all, to spend time with his mother. So he picked up a knife and got to work, peeling potatoes with her and his aunts in the kitchen.

'What are you doing, Sahibji? You're an officer now. You can't be peeling potatoes with us,' Iqra said as she tried to snatch the knife from Ummer.

'Being an officer means that you can't peel potatoes? No one ever said that to us at the academy,' Ummer joked. If only Ummer could tell Iqra what all they did in the academy. Peeling potatoes was quite respectable compared to that.

'So what do you do in the army? Are the officers in your unit as bad as they are here?' Ummer's sisters interrogated him.

They all had questions for him and he answered each one patiently even as he peeled the potatoes. Later, he went out and fetched everything that they needed for the next few days from the shops.

The following day was the mehendi ceremony. The house was full of music, light and happiness. All the women folk had their hands decorated in elaborate designs, and the mehendi slowly began to change into an auspicious dark orange.

Watching the women, Ummer thought of Tahzun and went up to the first floor to make a call to her. With the happy buzz of the wedding all around him, he wished intensely that Tahzun could be here with him. He couldn't get through to her.

Ummer called Uncle Manzoor in Anantnag and asked him to make haste and come to Batpora with his family. He then spoke to both his sisters.

'You have to come to the wedding this time. You didn't even come for Suby's wedding,' Ummer admonished Usma.

'Bhaiya, you know I hate weddings that involve our girl cousins and friends. Especially all the *rona-dhona* at the end,' said Usma.

'But this time, Musrat is not even leaving the house. They will both be staying here after the wedding, so it'll be a happy ending. You absolutely have to come!'

'Okay bhaiya, I'll be there with Asmat tomorrow evening, but you don't roam around outside. It's not safe there,' Usma said with much concern.

Just as he was making another call, three men with scarves covering their faces and shawl-wrapped bodies entered swiftly through the front door of the house. They climbed the stairs and threw open the door of the room that Ummer was sitting in. Jameela was in the bathroom attached to the same room.

'Are you Ummer Fayaz?' one of the men asked.

'Yes, I am,' Ummer replied, wondering who these intruders were. He knew it was rather late for guests to be visiting. He turned his wrist around out of sheer habit, and realized his watch was still at the repair shop, waiting for a new battery.

'Come with us!' another man commanded, exposing the gun under his shawl.

Hearing the commotion, Jameela hurried out of the bathroom. She was stunned into complete immobility at the sight of the guns the men were pointing at her son.

'Where do you want to take me?' Ummer asked.

'Just come with us. We need to talk to you,' the first man said.

Ummer got off the bed and put on his slippers, deliberately taking his time with them. He was trying to buy a few more minutes to assess the situation. But the men grew impatient and insisted that he hurry.

While they were heading upstairs, the intruders had hidden their guns under their shawls so the family assumed that they were Ummer's friends or colleagues. Only when they saw Ummer walking downstairs with them at gunpoint did they wake up to the gravity of the situation.

'Please don't take him,' Jameela pleaded with the second man.

The man turned around and hit Jameela in her stomach with the butt of his gun. Ummer tried to reach for his mother, but one of them drove the muzzle of his gun deeper into his back, showing that he meant business.

Jameela, who was doubled up on the floor in pain, got up again and pleaded with them, 'You are as good as sons to me. Just like my boy is my son. You are all sons of Kashmir. Please don't harm your brother. Just please take me along with you.'

But her pleas fell on deaf ears. By now, Ummer's instincts must have told him these were no ordinary men who wanted to chat with him on account of their differing ideologies. Not wanting to cause his family any further harm, he made it clear that he wouldn't resist.

'I'm coming with you. Please don't harm my family.' His voice was clear and firm. He started to walk ahead, making sure the men had to keep up with him and moved away from the family.

As they walked, the men didn't speak a word. There was no warning or explanation.

It was 8 p.m. when the three armed men took Ummer with them.

From here on, there is no available witness to what happened between them and Ummer.

Jameela and the other women were now weeping hysterically. Uncle Maqbool called Fayaz and apprised him of the situation.

'For God's sake, please call the police,' Jameela cried.

'Do you want to see your son dead? If we call the police, they will definitely kill him, Jameela,' Maqbool warned.

No one spoke after that as they were in shock, merely considering the possibility. The festive house suddenly wore a pall of gloom. Twenty-three years earlier, a heavily pregnant Jameela had arrived at her maternal home with Ummer warmly cocooned in her womb. And now he had been taken from the same house, perhaps never to return.

On the same night, DSP Ashiq Tak was returning from Behi Bagh to Shopian. As he approached Herman village, his vehicle came under heavy firing. It was only by a whisker that he made it out of there alive.

But an instinct born of experience told DSP Ashiq that the firing was a cover-up for some unusual terrorist activity in the area. He registered an FIR as soon as he reached the Shopian police station.

He was right. At around 6 a.m. the next morning, one of his inspectors called the DSP to inform him that a certain Lieutenant Ummer Fayaz had been found dead at Herman Chowk and that the body was presently at the Shopian District Hospital undergoing a post-mortem. He reached the hospital as fast as he could and discovered that the slain officer was Sarpanch Mushtaq's nephew.

The post-mortem pointed to gruesome torture before Ummer was shot multiple times. The injuries on his body revealed that he was subjected to beatings with sticks and the butt of a rifle. His back, legs and arms were targeted the most.

When Ummer's body was released after the examination, Shakeela and Manzoor tried to clean the blood off as best as they could. They didn't want Fayaz, Jameela or the girls to see him like that.

Ummer's mortal remains reached his home in Kulgam after the post-mortem at the district hospital. Asmat saw Ummer first. Taking slow steps towards his lifeless body, she stared at his face, disfigured by the bullet wound. It took a few seconds for her to register the evidence of her own eyes before she screamed and collapsed in unbelievable pain.

In compliance with Ummer's request the previous evening, Usma was all set to travel to Batpora for the wedding festivities. So when she saw that Uncle Manzoor had come to Anantnag to take her to Kulgam by cab, she knew instinctively that something was wrong. She suspected that she knew what the matter was, and blurted out to her uncle, 'It's Lalaji, isn't it? Is he still with us?' Usma said referring to her grandfather.

'He's just unwell, Beta,' said Manzoor, not having the strength to break the news to her and watch her disintegrate.

Usma feared the worst, that they had lost Grandpa. On reaching Kulgam, she saw a huge crowd outside their home. She flung open the cab door and ran into the house. Making her way to the body, her eyes took a moment to adjust to the fact that it was Ummer they were mourning. The shock of it made her pass out.

Javed and Zainub came as soon as they heard, and stayed with the family for a while to lend their support. But they were equally stunned by grief and shock. They had never imagined that one of them would die so young or in such macabre circumstances.

Ummer's army unit turned out in full strength to bid their comrade farewell and make sure he was buried with military honours. His body was shrouded in the national flag and carried by uniformed men to his resting place. As the sound of the bugle filled the air, Colonel Manu, along with some senior JCOs and jawans, slow-marched to Ummer and laid a wreath on his body. After the symbolic reversal of their weapons as a sign of homage to Ummer, they bowed their heads in silence for a few moments.

Towards the end, came the gun salute—a symbolic firing of three rounds into the air.

As the ceremonial salute came to a close, the tricoloured flag that had enfolded Ummer was carefully folded and handed over to Fayaz. For those mourning him, it seemed like an unfair barter; the national flag for a dead son.

Wrapped in a white *kafan*, Ummer was finally laid to rest. But what he left behind was untold distress and unrest.

The news flashes on national television were relentless, and the gruesome WhatsApp forwards were worse. Bhoi was somewhere in Arunachal Pradesh, learning the fine art of mine-laying, when he got one such miserable forward. It had to be a hoax, he thought. But just to be sure, he switched on the TV. The news channels were airing the rumour that a doctor had died in Shopian. So, of course, it wasn't Ummer, Bhoi told himself. He tried his friend's number, but couldn't get through.

But his relief was only temporary, for he soon received another WhatsApp forward with an image of Ummer's battered body. He made a few more calls and confirmed that it was no hoax. Devastated, he called Malik.

'I cannot believe this is happening, but it is true. I could do nothing for him,' said Bhoi, sobbing into the phone.

When they came to know of the circumstances under which he was killed, their grief turned to intense anger. Meanwhile, as Ummer's family received a steady stream of people who came to offer their condolences, the nation was also awakening to the news of this tragedy. Candlelight marches were held for Ummer throughout India, with large turnouts to pay homage to the young officer.

Majid comforted Bhoi over the phone.

'Sir, what good is this uniform I'm wearing if I couldn't protect him?'

'We couldn't protect him, Bhoi. But we will avenge him,' said Majid with a firmness in his voice.

They decided to volunteer with the Rashtriya Rifles after their six years of mandatory service. But the Indian Army couldn't wait that long. The job had to be done. Now. The message had to be sent. Now.

Lieutenant Colonel Inderjeet Singh was devastated. He shaved his head and asked Rajni, his wife, to help him perform all the rituals that they would have performed on the death of a family member.

Tahzun was inconsolable, racked with guilt over not having picked up his call on that fateful night. It was three days after his murder that she finally mustered the strength to visit Asmat and Usma.

The man at the repair shop, on hearing the news, had returned Ummer's watch to the sisters when he came to visit the family. Asmat and Usma thought it right that they hand it back to Tahzun.

The watch seemed to be biding its time, counting seconds off the lives of his killers with each tick. The army had already assured the family and the nation that they would bring the men responsible for the death of Lieutenant Ummer Fayaz to justice.

Epilogue

The task of nabbing the terrorists responsible for Ummer's death was now the responsibility of 34 RR. Their commanding officer was gathering intelligence but had been biding his time for the right opportunity. The ticking watch, the tears of the family and the anger of his comrades were finally given closure on 31 March 2018.

In Kachdoora, a small village in Shopian, those seeking justice for Ummer found an unlikely ally in Zeenat. Her son had been brutally murdered by the jihadis and her daughter, cruelly raped.

Zeenat learnt that five gun-toting terrorists were hiding in farmer Rayees Ahmed Bhat's home. They were also carrying ammunition and radio sets. She knew that life was giving her an opportunity to settle scores. There was nothing left to lose—her son was gone, and her daughter seemed to have lost her will to live. So she took the information that she had to the local police station.

In no time, police and army units in the area were abuzz with activity. The task force was now intercepting calls and checking with their own intelligence sources to confirm the information. Zeenat refused to budge from the police station until her tip-off was corroborated. She wanted to be sure that the authorities would act. When intelligence confirmed that these men were indeed the culprits they were looking for, the police told Zeenat she was going to be taken to an undisclosed safe location until the operation was over. Her identity as the informer would not be revealed. But that was the least of her concerns. She wanted the militants dead.

From the intercepted mobile calls, the police learnt that they had stumbled on to a gang of seven terrorists. In addition to the five men hiding in Bhat's house in Kachdoora, a few more were holed up in another location in Draggad district.

DSP Ashiq received a call at 10 p.m. from the adjutant of 34 RR. He was en route to Srinagar after arresting notorious ATM thieves. Knowing that prompt action was crucial, he took a diversion for Kachdoora immediately. The army had already laid out the outer cordon. At around 12.30 a.m., with the inner cordon also set up, they made the first announcement from the local masjid. Simultaneously, another unit was conducting a similar operation in Draggad district.

The announcements created panic and the terrorists started to fire. The army's first casualty was a gunner, Nealesh Singh. Amidst the commotion that followed, a terrorist managed to escape. But this helped the army zone in on the house that they had been hiding in.

The terrorists in Kachdoora took fourteen civilians hostage and refused to surrender. Not wanting to risk innocent lives, the officers leading the operation ordered a ceasefire. The terrorists were at an advantage at this point and the army lost two more jawans—Sepoy Het Ram and Gunner Arvind Kumar.

Being a local, DSP Ashiq knew the people and the area well. He roped in Hamid, a middle-aged man with a mobile phone. The DSP was strategically stationed just outside the outer cordon. He asked for the numbers of all the people on Hamid's phone and started to call them one by one, instructing them to get in touch with the other locals and evacuate the village.

He saved Bhat's number for the end. Bhat answered the call, saying that he was too terrified to leave the house with the other civilian hostages.

'If we do that sir, they will kill us,' Bhat pleaded, terror-stricken.

'Listen to me carefully, Bhat. We don't have much time. Send a woman and child out first.'

DSP Ashiq had served in Kashmir for a long time and understood the psyche of locals and terrorists alike. If the terrorists fired on innocent civilians, nothing would stop the locals from turning on them and retaliating.

A minute later, the silhouette of a woman and child became visible. They scurried out of the house and were led away by soldiers to the safe zone. One by one, DSP Ashiq managed to convince all fourteen hostages to walk out of the house. His gut instinct proved right; the terrorists were reluctant to fire at the locals.

Once all the civilians were safe, the army launched a no-holds-barred attack. The unit was already furious as they had lost three men in the operation. There was no holding them back now. As they opened fire on the house, some local supporters of the terrorists made their own announcements and gathered around the operation site to disrupt proceedings. As expected, stone-pelters got to work and the army had to stop firing intermittently, to make sure that the miscreants did not become casualties.

The crossfire continued until late noon. Initially, until about 10 a.m., the army had gone slow in the hope that the terrorists would surrender. Then they intensified their efforts. Eventually, a bullet hit a gas cylinder inside the house, causing a huge explosion. Within minutes, the house was reduced to smouldering debris.

Combing through the ruins, they were able to confirm that all five terrorists including the two who had killed Ummer—Ishfaq Ahmad Thokar and Ghyssul Islam—had perished in the explosion. They had been reduced to ashes, and no one who was alive could confirm whether they had reached Jannat in the name of jihad.

On the morning of 1 April 2018, I heard the news. I sat with my eyes glued to the TV, wanting to be sure of it. When the reports were confirmed, I felt an overwhelming sense of relief. Ummer's sister Asmat called. She knew that I had been waiting for that day, as much as her family was. We shed tears as we spoke about him on the phone.

'I heard that one fellow escaped.' Asmat was still a little disappointed.

'Don't worry, Asmat! He will also meet his dead friends soon,' I assured her. And it was only a few months later on 25 November 2018 that 34 RR conducted another operation where five militants along with Mohd Abbas Bhatt was killed.

Finally, we had closure.

* * *

There was one person who had been a vital source of support throughout my research on Ummer Fayaz, and I was due to meet him the day after.

Neeraj Kumar has helped me in innumerable ways from the beginning of the project to its end. I wanted to now make sense of all the information I had, and I knew I could count on him to guide me.

'Why did you choose to write about Lieutenant Ummer Fayaz?' Mr Kumar asked.

I wondered if I had chosen the story or if the story had chosen me. I had admired Ummer's courage of conviction and the life choices he had made against great odds, even though they had sped him towards his death. It was a story that was begging to be told.

And then I looked around the coffee shop that we were seated in. I wondered if the people who were sipping on their cappuccinos, smiling and laughing with friends and family, and generally enjoying their day, knew Lieutenant Ummer Fayaz.

Mr Kumar was taken aback when I rose from my chair and walked up to a complete stranger to ask if he knew Lieutenant Ummer Fayaz. It turned out that he didn't.

And from the look on his face, it appeared that he didn't care either.

I walked up to another person and asked him the same question. I repeated the process at a few other tables in the coffee shop until I finally found someone who had heard his name. That brought a smile to my face. But I had also answered Mr Kumar's question.

I'm sure some people in the coffee shop that day assumed that I was not of sound mind. But that is of little consequence when we consider the fact that the nation remains largely unaware of the insanity that has engulfed Kashmir, claiming precious lives almost every other day.

Since Ummer was kidnapped and killed on 9 May 2017, five similar deaths have occurred:

- Muhammad Ayub Pandith (DSP, Srinagar), lynched by a mob on 22 June 2017
- Ramzan Parray (Constable, BSF), killed at home in Bandipora on 27 September 2017
- Irfan Ahmad Dar (Rifleman, Territorial Army), abducted and murdered while on leave in his hometown in Shopian on 25 November 2017
- Aurangzeb (Rifleman, 44 RR) of Pulwama, abducted and murdered on 14 June 2018
- Javid Ahmad Dar (Constable, J&K Police, Kulgam), abducted and murdered on 5 July 2018
- Jawan Hilal Ahmad Bhat (Territorial Army) went missing on 8 October from Shah. His bullet-riddled body was recovered from the Sanglan forest area in Utrasoo, Anantnag

There are always three versions of any event—yours, mine, and the actual truth. I was hoping to tell the truth about the life and death of Lieutenant Ummer Fayaz, and I believe I have done my best.

Ummer died while serving a cause that he deeply believed in, that of defending the nation from those who would harm it. He fought his battle and died before his time. He has left us now with choices to make. Whose side are we on?

I had been waiting for a fitting conclusion for this book ever since it was conceptualized. I thought I had got an end to the book when all the terrorists who had kidnapped and murdered him were killed.

But the perfect ending remains elusive. The day no author has to dip his or her pen in the blood that flows unabated in the Valley to write its stories, that would be the day that is worthy of a perfect ending. Until then, long live Kashmir!

Scan QR code to access the
Penguin Random House India website